Dahnmon's Little Stories

Dahnmon's Little Stories

Colonel Charles Dahnmon Whitt

Jesse Stuart Foundation
Ashland, Kentucky 2010

Dahnmon Whitt Family

Published May 27, 2010

First Edition Copyright by Colonel Charles Dahnmon Whitt
All rights reserved. No part of this book may be reproduced or utilized in any form or by any means with out permission in writing from the publisher.

Published By:
Jesse Stuart Foundation
1645 Winchester Avenue
Ashland, KY 41101
606 326 1667 jsfbooks.com   http://dahnmonwhittfamily.com

COLONEL CHARLES DAHNMON WHITT

Dahnmon's Little Stories

Chapters

Page 3	*The Bird On The Clothes Line*
Page 6	*The First Trout I Ever Caught*
Page 11	*Brave Bear Hunter*
Page 17	*Fishing With Uncle Gene*
Page 21	*Raising Rabbits In Raven*
Page 25	*My First Big Trout*
Page 31	*Camping With Dad and My Big Brothers*
Page 37	*A Tsunami On Straight Creek*
Page 43	*Working On The World Trade Center*
Page 52	*Inside A Jet Plane, Didn't Know If I Would Get Out Again*
Page 57	*Helping Big Brother With His Paper Route*
Page 60	*Nails And Boards*
Page 64	*A New Year*
Page 65	*What Price*

COLONEL CHARLES DAHNMON WHITT

Dahnmon's Little Stories

Page 67   *The Scare On High Knob*

Page 70   *How Did I Get Here*

Page 73   *What Is A Creek?*

Page 76   *My Motel Adventures*

Page 81   *Young Aviation*

Page 86   *What The Flag Means To Me*

Page 89   *Son Of A Coal Miner*

Page 92   *Truitt Grist Mill*

Page 97   *Big White Oak Creek Of Greenup County Kentucky*

Page 99   *Tecumseh Stomps His Foot*

Page 114   *About The Author*

Page 117   *Picture Of The Old Colonel*

COLONEL CHARLES DAHNMON WHITT

Dahnmon's Little Stories

The Bird On The Clothes Line

For my twelfth birthday, Mom gave me a Daisy Defender BB Gun, with certain stipulations. I had to agree not to shoot at any birds. I agreed spontaneously so I could get my hands on the new air rifle. The Daisy Defender was a special model; it had a magazine like the pump models and only held fifty BB's. It was also more powerful than most air rifles.

"Now son, if I ever hear of you shooting birds I will take your BB gun, and you will never get it back," Mommy told me.

"I promise, I won't shoot birds," I answered quickly.

"Here is your birthday present, please be careful with it," Mommy said as she handed me the most precious gift a boy could get.

I took the new air rifle everywhere I went during the next few days, and did not even think of shooting at any live targets. As time went on I became quiet proficient with the great little rifle. All the boys were envious of my treasure. I could shoot farther and more accurate than any of my friends.

After several months passed the temptation grew, and I yielded. My neighbors the Kennedy's, saved scraps of food for their hogs. They had a bucket hanging at the end of their clothes line. We called it a slop bucket back then. The bucket was up out of reach of dogs, cats, and other critters that may want to feed upon the enticing morsels. The bucket did attract a long line of black birds that lined up on the clothes line. This was my temptation, and one day I could not resist.

I had to be stealth, not to get a shot at the

COLONEL CHARLES DAHNMON WHITT

Dahnmon's Little Stories

birds, but not to get caught. This day only one black bird set on the line close to the slop bucket. I looked at my house, my grand mother's house and round about for any witness that may report an unauthorized shooting. The coast was clear so I took the opportunity to try my air rifle on a living, breathing bird.

I gave one more, quick look around, raised the rifle and aimed at the feathered target. I squeezed the trigger and the deadly missile was on the way. What happened next was unbelievable; I hit the black bird in the head and killed it instantly. It didn't fall to the ground; it had a death grip on the clothes line and just hung there upside down, as evidence of my mischief. The bird kept swinging back and forward to torment me.

I panicked, I had to get that bird to turn loose of the clothes line and hide the evidence. I laid down my prized weapon and ran in a bolt toward the swinging bird. I jumped up and hit the bird with my hand to knock it down, and this only caused it to swing round and round.

Oh my, this bird was determined to reek revenge on its slayer. What was I going to do? I jumped with all my might with both hands extended and caught the bird with a death grip. With all my weight and might I yanked the bird free of the clothes line. I threw the dead thing over in the weeds to hide the evidence. I looked all around and as far as I could tell, no one saw this crime but Almighty God.

I was instantly sorry for my actions, it was the first thing I ever killed, and I was sorry about that. I was also sorry for breaking my promise to Mommy. My crime was hidden; I would just have to live with it.

COLONEL CHARLES DAHNMON WHITT

Dahnmon's Little Stories

Almost fifty years later when Mommy was in poor health and not too long for this world, I confessed the whole thing to her. She smiled and said you have been punished enough by keeping this secret for all of these years. I knew I was forgiven, and felt relieved for killing the swinging black bird. I can still see that bird hanging upside down and swinging back and forth, in my mind.

This one got away!

COLONEL CHARLES DAHNMON WHITT

Dahnmon's Little Stories

The First Trout I Ever Caught

I remember it like it was yesterday, that first wiggly Trout I had in my slick hands. It all started the year before when I was a first grader. Trout season opened in western Virginia at noon in early April. Back then People in the area would take off work to enjoy the stocked mountain streams in the western counties. My Dad did not miss work very much but he must have really enjoyed the annual opening day of trout season. I remember as he prepared to go fishing that day, I wanted to go with him so bad. He knew the mountain terrain and rugged trout streams were not the place for a first grader on opening day. Even though I put up a demanding performance of tears and pleading I was left behind. Dad did halfway promise that I could go the next year.

Dad left with his store bought cane pole and seemed to be gone forever. I waited with great anticipation for his return, because I knew he would have some of the beautiful Rainbow Trout for me to look at and even eat, even though I did not like fish too much.

Sure enough when Dad got home he had three of the most beautiful fish I ever saw. I remember them as really big, but like everything else, things are big to a first grader. I was so proud of Dad's accomplishment, and just knew I could catch some if I just had a chance.

Back to my fish story, Dad did let me go when I was in the second grade. It was a beautiful spring day as I remember it. I was all excited and had my little green pole that Dad cut from the brush along the way. He attached the black fishing line

Dahnmon's Little Stories

about half way down the pole. Then he tied it again at the very top of the green sapling. He explained that if a fish broke my pole he would still be tied at the center. Dad was very smart like that.

Dad packed us some sandwiches and stuff in a brown bag, got our night crawlers, and we headed for Wolf Creek. This is some of the most rugged country in Virginia.

Dad told me to be really careful because of the rough conditions, but I thought I was a tough boy in the second grade. When we got to Wolf Creek Dad let me fish by myself, but he stayed close so he could do a rescue if he needed to.

The little leafs were just starting to grow and the mountain Dogwoods were blooming. There was much greenery even this early in the spring due to the Mountain Laurel, and Hemlocks. The rocks were so slick, as if God had given them a greasing. As soon as we left the car I started a trend for the day, fall down and get up. Dad thought it was funny, but still was afraid I would get hurt.

"Now Son, be careful, if you get hurt we will have to go home," Dad said.

I had what they call fisherman's luck, "A wet tail and a hungry gut."

Now back then the season did not open until twelve noon, so we all got our tackle ready, and had a bite to eat. Then we put on a night crawler and waited for the magical hour to drop our baits to the awaiting trout. The game wardens were walking up and down the banks disguised as fishermen trying to catch somebody dropping a hook in too early. They wore fishing clothes and had flies on their hats. Dad pointed them out to me and warned me not to start too early. He said to watch him, and when he started fishing for me to start also. I could hardly wait.

Dahnmon's Little Stories

Finally we were fishing in earnest along with about every other men and boys in the western end of Virginia. People were getting their lines tangled with each other, and some were slipping and sliding almost as much as me.

People started yanking out the flopping fish and I even got a bite or two. I was too slow to hook the sneaky things. Dad had three or four nice trout and I still had not caught my first.

I did the forbidden thing in fishing, I moved in on two fellers that were having really good luck. They gave me a dirty look but didn't say anything. I baited up and flipped my worm out among the hungry trout and sure enough one wanted it. I yanked on the little green pole and the trout landed right in my hands against my chest. The wrestling match was on as I tried to hold on to the slippery Rainbow Trout. As I remember it, it was a big one, but I lost the battle, it was free once again in Wolf Creek.

I was exasperated at giving my prized catch its freedom, and just stood there for a long moment. I remember I started to trudge to the bank to get another worm, but one of the fishermen gave me another worm so I would just be still. I didn't get another fish that year, but I felt some comfort in knowing I had a whopper in my hands. Remember what I said about things looking big when you are a kid!

The day went fast and it was time to go home. Dad had six nice sized fish and we headed to the car. I was totally worn out after fighting the rough ground, slick rocks and a whopper trout. Dad consoled me and said there would be other trips. He explained that I needed a landing net, even though he had none of his own. Sure enough the next year

Dahnmon's Little Stories

came and I was there with my new landing net. Guess what, I caught not one trout, but two. Dad and I never missed an opening day of trout season until I left for the Navy.

Dahnmon's Little Stories

"I Got One!"

COLONEL CHARLES DAHNMON WHITT

Dahnmon's Little Stories

Brave Bear Hunter

My first real deer hunt brought out some doubts, fears, and bravery. It all took place in the Carroll County Virginia Mountains. I was with an older friend by the name of Reece. I was about sixteen and Reece was in his upper forties. I had met him while I worked at the Raven Super Market.

Reece was a typical redneck, and had built a forerunner to the modern truck camper. It was a plywood contraption build on his old pickup. He had two beds and a little laundry stove for heat. I thought it was all built masterfully. The day came, a Sunday morning, and we headed out across Route 16, and across the three high mountains to Marion, Virginia. To a flatlander, this is scarier than a ride on the biggest roller coaster ever made. Reece drove carefully up each mountain, using a lot of gas, (27 cents per gallon) then he would shut off the engine and coast all the way to the bottom. I was just too youthful to be afraid of such tactics.

We left on Sunday, which gave us time to set up camp and scout out a place to hunt on Monday morning when the Deer Season actually opened. Virginia was really strict about its game laws and also speed limits in the early sixties. We kept our rifles and shot guns in their cases on Sunday, they had already been checked out, fired and cleaned the week before.

We got over to the Carroll County Mountains and set up Reece's prized camper by pulling one side up on a rock to level her out. Then after eating some bologna sandwiches we went out into the woods and staked out a spot for in the morning. During the day we ran into some other

Dahnmon's Little Stories

hunters from our little village of Raven, VA One of them had just bought an International Scout, a nifty little four wheel drive. They didn't have four wheelers back in the early sixties. I ran into Jack the owner of the Scout a day later, he was straddle a log down in the woods, and could not get the front wheels locked in. I helped him rock it a bit and he finally got the front locked in and climbed across the log.

The night before we went into the woods for the first hunt we checked out our licenses, and I noticed that I had a bear tag as well as a deer tag. Reece told me that there were bears in these mountains, and if I saw one it was fair game. This made me think about the possibility of bringing home a bear. I knew that bears are dangerous critters, and you better have a good shot if you wanted to bag one. The old saying rings true, "Sometimes you get the bear, and sometimes the bear gets you!"

Now for my Rifle, It was a small cannon. I had purchased it from Sears by mail order for $10.88. It was a surplus British 303. This was before the laws had changed, due to the assassination of President Kennedy. The only stipulation was that Sears did not sell to miners. Dad had given me permission to order the big rifle. A year or two earlier I wanted to get one, but I read that they did not sell to miners. I asked Day why he couldn't order a rifle. Dad was a coal miner, why would they discriminate against miners I questioned? Dad had a good laugh on that one.

Well anyway, I had this big gun that held ten bullets in the clip and one in the chamber. The bullets were rated bigger that the American 30-06 and had 215 grain bullets. Shucks, if I could hit it, it

Dahnmon's Little Stories

would bring down an elephant. So I felt confident about having fire power even for a big bear.

The next morning we were up hours before sunrise, ate a hurried breakfast as we warmed by the little laundry stove. We put on several layers of warm clothing to ward off the below freezing mountain air. Next we took our flashlights and headed out toward our deer stands. It was exciting as we noticed flashlights all around the mountains, the hunters lights reminded us of fireflies as they headed to a place to hunt. The trails did not look anything like they did in the light of the day before. About first light the high powered rifles and shot guns began to rang out. I heard one that reminded me of someone tearing overall britches. If you heard one shot, usually it would be followed by one or two more as the deer ran past numerous hunters. I still had limited visibility; it is always darker in the mountain woods. I could hear deer running but never saw a one that morning. The season was for bucks only, but I think that many of the crazy hunters were shooting at anything that moved. Some of the hunters were hung over from a night of drinking and poker playing. As I sat there watching the fog freeze on my rifle barrel, I realized why deer hunting was so dangerous. I did see a scared doe up in the day as she was hauling the mail right toward me; I began to wonder if she was going to run right over me. She saw me as I began to move out of the way, and she did a 180 degree turn in midair.

Next day went about the same, except I saw many squirrels playing in the trees. After lunch on the second day I pulled out my 1948 Topper H & R twenty gauge shotgun and killed a squirrel for supper. After supper we sat around talking and planning the hunt for the third and last day of our

Dahnmon's Little Stories

hunt. Reece thought we might be better off hunting over on the other ridge, which we had not even been on. We had no time to explore; we would be traveling in unknown woods with only our little flash lights to illuminate the sparse trails. The mountains had an abundance of Laurel and thickets. We trudged along until the trail split, Reece took the one to the right and I took the left which leveled off slightly. It was pitch dark at this parting, but I could see the sky lightening up way off in the East by the coming dawn. It was like being in another world.

    I traveled about one third of a mile up the slightly rising trail. Each minute that passed brought a little more light to the mountain.

    I started looking for a place to have my stand, and found a rotting log that had been torn apart by some strong force. As I shined my light to investigate, a great big bear track stood out, in the loose dirt. I looked closer to realize that a bear had torn open the rotting log to feed upon the bugs and worms it held. My heart jumped and fluttered a little bit to the realization that I was in the dark woods with a big bear.

    It was still too dark to really get a good aim with the old 303. I began to scan the area around me. I turned 360 degrees slowly looking hard into the dim woods. I looked again at the dismantled log and bear tracks. I looked around and to the right slightly behind me, and about fifty yards up the ridge I saw something that made my heart jump again. My Lord, there is that big black bear I thought. It was just standing there looking toward the new morning light.

    What to do? What to do? Should I wait for more light? Should I sneak back down the trail, or should I start a stalking hunt and shoot this trophy

Dahnmon's Little Stories

with my big rifle? It was still a little too dark to aim through the conventional sights on the old British 303. Was I scared?

Yes I was scared, but I began to compose myself, and was quite pleased with the prospect of going home to Raven with a big bear. I thought about my fire power, and the ever increasing light. "Be brave," I told myself.

I began to stalk the big black thing, I moved like a Cherokee Brave through the dim woodland. I carefully placed each foot, not to break a twig or rattle the leaves on the woodland floor. It was still too dark for a long shot, I knew I had to get really close, or have much more light to let off a round from the big 303. My adrenaline was rushed about as far as it could go. I gripped the big rifle and quietly took of the safety. I had covered more ground than I realized, then I looked about again. It was getting much lighter now which relieved me to know I could aim much better now. I was only about fifteen yards from the black form waiting for me. With the added light of the new dawn and my closeness, I strained my every fiber to see the big bear.

Oh my, it was not a bear at all; it was an ancient black stump. I felt really weird, bewildered, and relieved at the same time. I felt foolish, yet really proud to know that I could face the giant bear, even though it was just a stump. It looked like a bear in the dim light of the Carroll County woods. Sure enough, there had been a bear about!

Dahnmon's Little Stories 16

**COLONEL CHARLES DAHNMON 16
WHITT**

Dahnmon's Little Stories

Fishing With Uncle Gene

When I was around eight years of age, My Uncle David Eugene took an interest in my fishing education. I was all for the new experience, and learned the love of fishing.

At the back of our home place, God put a creek. It was called Mill Creek, because at one time there was a grist mill at the base of a natural water falls. About one quarter of a mile down the little creek it ran into the Clinch River. This creek became a place of many hours of pleasure for me as I grew up. Above the creek on the other side was a steep hill, we called it a mountain when I was a kid. It was also a place of adventure, I may tell about it in a later tale.

Just at the corner of Dad's lots on the upstream side was the dirt and gravel road and a bridge that crossed Mill Creek. This was the first place I dropped a worm that I can remember. There was mostly Creek Minnows (I called them Minners) in it, but in the spring the Horny Heads migrated up stream to lay eggs I reckon. At any rate the big minnow like fish, with little knots on their heads, was headed up Mill Creek. When I said big, I meant big for minnows. It was fun to catch the shaking things.

Uncle Gene came and we got some garden worms and went way down the creek close to the Clinch that first time. The creek made a good turn and there was a hole against the bank. The creek was only eight to ten feet wide at this section. Gene baited up the little hook and tossed it over in the moving water and something took off with it. Gene gave a quick jerk and missed the little fish, but he

Dahnmon's Little Stories

caught its lips. We looked at the bare hook that had little fishy lips hanging on it. We laughed at the site, and Uncle Gene said, "Guess I jerked a little hard!"

We went fishing several times that summer, as time went by. I was introduced to seining and crawdad catching. I learned about hellgrammites the wormy little creature with a bunch of legs and a deadly pincher on the front end. Uncle Gene said, "They are good for small mouth bass, guess they turn into some kind of bug when they grow up and get out of the water."

I also learned about the sneaky snakes that played in the creek and even in the river. I learned about the plant that loved the banks of creeks and rivers in Virginia. You guessed it, Poison Oak, that green three leafed devil plant that loved to make blisters on unsuspecting boys like me. Yes, I got a good dose of it that summer. I learned to look for the hateful stuff.

Before the summer was gone we had gone to the Clinch many times, fishing with worms, minnows, crawdad tails, and oh yes hellgrammites. I was afraid of the twisty, pinching, "Hellesimites," as I called them. I found out my favorite fish to catch was the vicious little fighter, the Red Eye. If they were to grow to ten pounds a feller just couldn't land one. They were so aggressive, tearing worms from the hook and almost yanking the little green sapling from my hands.

When we got back with the fish, I had to help clean the fish. This was not much fun as they were slick, scaled and had guts you had to cut out. They also had prickly spines in there fins that loved to stick you when you tried to hold them.

Sometimes we would go seining at the creek falls which had a natural trough at the bottom, and

Dahnmon's Little Stories

the minnows were usually thick in this two feet of water. One day Uncle Gene sat the burlap seine at one end and I was supposed to wade while trashing and making a commotion to scare the miners into the seine. Only thing, there was a snake hanging on the falls sticking it's head right at me. No way was I going to scare minnows when that thing was there. Uncle Gene pleaded while being bent over holding the seine.

"Come on Dahnmon, scare the minners this way ," he said.

"I ain't going to do it!" I answered.

Uncle Gene stood up and took a handle of the seine and hit at that old creek snake and it swam right in front of me to the deeper hole to my left and on down the creek.

Uncle Gene was a patient young man, but he was a little exasperated after that.

"Now are you going to scare the miners to me?" he asked.

I waded on in the hole shifting my feet and dancing my way right up to the seine. Uncle Gene raised the burlap sack trap and we had a bunch of the little fishes we call minners. Red Eyes and small mouth bass love the little minnows.

I never caught any whoppers with Uncle Gene, but I did learn a lot about fishing and baiting and even cleaning fish. I learned about being around water and the great outdoors around my home in Tazewell County, Va. Mill Creek, and the Clinch River held many adventures back in the early fifties. I learned names like the Curve, Dixon Hole, and the Bridge, (N & W Railroad Bridge, crossed Mill Creek as it ran beside the Clinch River) the Swinging Bridge, and the Red Eye Hole.

One other thing I learned, or maybe it came

Dahnmon's Little Stories

natural like, I learned to tell fish stories.

I think Uncle Gene was back from the Army and taking the summer off before he tied himself down to anything. Dad worked every day at the mine and Gene was free to fish that summer. He has always been my favorite Uncle, and I made a lot of memories that summer. Funny thing was I did not like to eat the fish we caught. I love fish today, and love Uncle Gene.

Dahnmon's Little Stories

Raising Rabbits In Raven

I was around ten years old when Dad let me purchase a pet rabbit from the Joyce boys. They were our neighbors not too far away. The Joyce boys were my friends and enemies, according to what day it was. But that is another story. Now back to the Bunny Tale.

I got chicken wire and built a pen, and also a cage up off the ground with hardware cloth in the bottom. This was in there so when my rabbit did his business the little pellets fell out on the ground. I learned that from the Joyce boys.

As time went by, my Pete grew up and he was a girl rabbit, to my surprise. The Joyce boys told me I should bring her out for a visit and let her get bred, that way I could have little baby bunnies for sale. The idea sounded pretty good to me, so I took her courting out at the Joyce boys' house. I did not bother to ask Dad, I just knew he would like the idea. If I sold the new babies I could give him some money for feed and pen making stuff.

I found out, rabbits get their babies real quick, about three weeks. Somehow I got it in my head that mommy rabbits always have babies in increments of seven. I don't remember how I learned this important thing, dreamed it or maybe the Joyce boys.

I told Dad that I took Pete courting, and he was not as pleased about it as I was. I told him that Pete would have seven babies before long.

"Now you don't know she will have seven babies!" Dad said.

"When did you take her out there?" he asked.

Dahnmon's Little Stories

"About two weeks ago I reckon, and yes she will get seven babies," I said insistently.

Dad just shook his head and smiled as if to say, "Wait and see."

Now you have to picture this, Dad bought all the fencing, boards, and nails, not to mention food for my rabbit. Now she was going to be a mommy rabbit.

The short gestation period for rabbits is only three weeks and it past quickly. I went out one morning and Pete had dug a hole under a board in the floor of the pen. She had pulled all the fur off her chest and had lost substantial weight. I investigated the situation and was pleased to be the owner of seven new bunny babies. I couldn't wait for Dad to get home from work to tell him the good news. I also wanted him to know that mommy rabbits do always have seven babies the first time.

When Dad got home that evening in his normal coal dirty clothes and black face, I ran to greet him and tell about Pete having babies.(Dad was a coal miner)

"Dad, Pete had seven babies just like I told you," I said proudly.

"She did, now that is just a coincidence that she had seven," Dad replied.

After Dad had his bath and eat supper Mom, and Dad went out to see Pete's babies.

"They sure are cute little things," mommy said.

I agreed and reemphasized that she had seven just like I said.

Even Mommy agreed with Daddy, rabbits don't always have seven babies the first time. Didn't Pete just prove that they do, I thought.

Dahnmon's Little Stories

Time went on and the babies grew up quickly. The Joyce boys suggested I bring Pete courting again. It sounded like a splendid idea; I could picture the fourteen new bunny babies in my young mind.

Dad had not complained about buying rabbit food for the now eight rabbits I had. After I took Pete courting again I told Dad about the new development and that Pete was expecting fourteen new baby bunnies. Dad did not share the excitement and anticipation that I did. Now Dad disagreed with me again about how many babies mommy rabbits have.

Sometimes Mommies and Daddies seem so dumb, I thought.

Daddy implied he would not be too happy with all the new little mouths to feed. Fourteen I knew.

In no time at all Pete got fat and pulled the fur off her chest again. I went out one morning to find Pete had babies again. I pulled out all the new little arrivals and counted each one. Guess what, she had fourteen new bunny babies. As before I could hardly wait to tell Daddy when he got home from the mine. As soon as he got home I ran to tell him of the grand news. (Mother rabbit's line their nest with the fur from their chest.)

"Pete had babies last night," I told with much pride.

"How many did she have?" Daddy asked as if to prove a point.

"Fourteen," I said proudly.

"Don't you know that mommy rabbits always have fourteen babies the second time?" I asked as a pro rabbit breeder.

"That is just a coincidence," Daddy insisted.

Dahnmon's Little Stories

Now Pete had proved that mommy rabbits always have fourteen the second time, not to mention that she proved they have seven the first time. After a couple of weeks passed I mentioned that Pete would have twenty one babies next time.

"Oh No, she wouldn't, you are not taking Pete courting any more," Dad said in no uncertain terms.

I now had twenty two rabbits, guess what, Dad wanted me to get ride of some of my baby bunnies.

I guess me and Pete finally convinced Daddy that mommy rabbits have babies in increments of seven!

COLONEL CHARLES DAHNMON WHITT

Dahnmon's Little Stories

My First Big Trout

Once upon a time when I was around fourteen I had a covenant with Dad! I could go fishing on Sunday afternoon with Doug and his Grand Paw John, after I got out of church. I always made it a point to go to The Raven Methodist Church where Dad was the Sunday school Superintendent and Lay Leader. He thought it to be important for me to be in church every Sunday. I thought it was very important for me to go fishing with John and Doug most every Sunday. So we came to an understanding, I went to church and John would pick up Doug and myself shortly thereafter.

John was a coal miner and loved the weekend. He was one of the most proficient fishermen I ever knew. If only one fish was caught, you could bet John would be the one that did the catching. He would take Doug and I and head out to Little Tumbling Creek, Little River, Cedar Creek, Clear Fork and numerous other mountain streams in southwest Virginia.

This beautiful summer day, Eugene, Doug's daddy decided to go and wet a line with us. We hurriedly got our tackle together and got into John's Red 1957 four door hardtop Chevy and traveled through the beautiful countryside of Tazewell County. We made small talk about this and that, and before long we were crossing the little woodland bridge over Little Tumbling Creek. After parking and getting our gear out, John told us he was going to fish down stream from the bridge to the little country church about a mile away. He liked fishing by himself so us younger angler's would not be any determent in his fishing. Eugene was stuck with

Dahnmon's Little Stories

Doug and I, we headed upstream.

The water in Little Tumbling was so clear that in a pool of about five feet, the bottom could be viewed clearly as if it was one foot deep. Of course in the eddies, the glare of moving water obscured what ever might be there. Eugene was a good fisherman and not to brag, but Doug and I were not too shabby for boys. We had caught a number of fish in the past few years. John would just say, "we were lucky."

This particular day was a hot day but the trees that shaded both sides of the mountain stream kept us cool. The only draw back to hot weather is that it slows the feeding trout to a standstill. Trout love cold water and thrive on feeding frenzies of flies and hatchlings around the creek. We fished our way up the Little Tumbling for about four hours and none of us had a trout to show for it. We had all three had a hit or two but caught none. We started back toward the Chevy, hitting a hole or two as we worked our way down stream. We talked some and speculated some as to how many fish John caught. Doug and I figured the old pro had to have a couple even on this slow day. Eugene said, "I doubt that John has a fish, considering the action we had."

The shadows were getting pretty long by the time we got back to the car. John was still somewhere down the creek fishing his heart out. Eugene and Doug found themselves a good seat for the wait. I walked over on the bridge and looked deeply into the shadowy waters on the upstream side then on the downstream side. I did not see a fish, but I noticed a big root on the left bank that strutted out into a pool of slow moving water. I thought that to be a prime spot, for mister trout to hide out. I made my way across the little country

Dahnmon's Little Stories

bridge and down on to the bank where the root stuck out over the water. I approached slowly and went close to the water, hiding myself from the water with the big tree.

I slowly stuck my head around the tree and peered into the pool just behind the great root. What I saw made my heart stop, and then flutter like a butterfly. I saw a big trout rise up near the top of the water to investigate something floating by. I backed off into the cover behind the tree so as not to alarm my unsuspecting quarry. I thought for a minute as to what kind of bait I should present to this big boy. I couldn't decide if salmon eggs or a night crawler would be best. I decided to put on both, a whole worm with only about 1 inch threaded on the number four hook, and then I strung on three salmon eggs. I looked the bait over and surmised that the big trout would like the looks of my presentation.

I moved toward the pool from behind the tree, and my dangling crawler latched on to a tall weed. I patiently got it un-hung and got myself into the best position to drop the bait. I slowly dipped the worm and eggs into the most favorable spot to attract the big boy. I moved the end of the pole back and forth while I patiently waited. I didn't wait too long. I saw the shadowy figure that reminded me of a submarine rising for the bait. Now don't jerk too quickly I thought. He had it and my line drew tight, I gave it a yank spontaneously and he was hooked. He kept trying to head under the roots of the tree, but I kept him out of that trap. I worked him up stream and flipped him out on the bank where I fell on him like a bird on a June bug. By now I knew you had to get a finger through a gill to hold a slippery trout. I got him pinned down and my right

Dahnmon's Little Stories

finger next to my thumb on my right hand through the mouth and gill. He had little teeth chewing on me as I gathered my stringer and strung him onto it. I was sure I had him on the stringer before I yelled at Doug. He was big and thick for a trout, I figured him to be two feet long, but to a kid fisherman, everything appears bigger. At any rate he was a nice one.

I proudly carried him back across the bridge where Doug and even Eugene hurried to meet me. There eyes were big as they viewed my beauty.

Eugene said, "Nice fish, they will hit anything at about dark."

I didn't answer because I didn't feel like I took unfair advantage of him by the dimming light.

John comes up the bank at about that time and he had one little trout in his creel. He took one look at my fish and asked how I caught it. All the way home we talked about my fish and how I caught it.

"I never heard of anybody fishing with a whole night crawler and three salmon eggs at one time," John went on.

"Me neither, but it works I reckon," I answered.

"Well you got the fish to prove it," said John.

When we got home I thanked John for the fishing trip gave him two dollars for gas, and ran into the house to show off my fish to Dad. He and Mommy were excited to see my big trout.

"Reckon how big it is?" I asked.

"You all never measured it?" Dad asked.

"No, we didn't have any thing to measure with," I answered.

Dad laid it out on the counter and took a

Dahnmon's Little Stories

tape measure from the tip of the tail to the end at the mouth. Now remember things look bigger to kids. It was a real nice fish but not a giant. As trout go around the streams of Virginia it was big. Are you ready?

It measured fifteen inches. I was a little disappointed, but Dad said, "That is a big trout son."

I was so proud of my fish, I hated to clean it and shorten it by cutting off its head. Dad was always so smart about such things; he came up with a good plan that would allow me to show off the fish for some time to come. He took a sharp knife and slit its belly and gently removed its guts, and left the head on for now. He wrapped it up in aluminum foil and placed it into the family freezer. Now any one that came by, I could run and get my trout out and tell the fish story.

The agreement that Dad held me too, about going to church was really the best. I didn't know it at the time, but since I look back and realize what I learned about my Jesus Christ is worth it all. As I said Dad was a smart man, he was also very wise and wanted to show me the truth and way to everlasting life.

I am also thankful for John Lawson, he always allowed me on his many fishing trips. If you have a boy there are two things you should teach him, fishing and going to church.

Dahnmon's Little Stories

COLONEL CHARLES DAHNMON WHITT

Dahnmon's Little Stories

Camping With Dad And My Big Brothers

I was very young, about six I reckon! I think the year was 1952. Larry my big brother got me to go to the garden with him. Jerry was going about getting other things ready. Daddy would be getting home from a hard day at the mine on a Friday evening and all was set for the four of us to have a three day camp on Holston Lake.

Larry was 5 years older than me and Jerry was two years older than Larry. At any rate I was ready to fish, as was my brothers. A lot of thought had gone into this trip, but I was just a little follower. Dad had agreed to take us on this great adventure and had told Jerry and Larry what to do while he was at work that day.

I was with Dad and my brothers a day or two before when Dad drove all three of us to a friend's home in Doran, a couple of miles from our Raven Virginia home on Mill Creek. Jerry or Larry had found out that a friend Billy had a tent that he would loan us for the outing. Now we had the tent with only half the pegs but we could make the rest out of sticks.

We were in the garden digging potatoes to eat on the trip. It must have been in late summer because potatoes were ready to dig. I can't remember all the details, but I guess Larry was graveling to get out the young spuds without hurting the vines. My job was to pick them up and put them in a box or poke.

I did think it odd that we would be taking potatoes to eat on a camping trip, but I had not given it much thought as to what you are suppose to eat while camping. Hotdogs were always my first choice back then. I do remember that we ate lots of potatoes on that trip; we even ate them for breakfast. Now days that are not a rare thing to have home fries for breakfast, but we had camp fries.

Dad had bought new fishing line and reed poles for Jerry and Larry. I still had my little green sapling with black fishing line that Dad had attached for me. The new fishing line that Dad, Jerry, and Larry were to use was almost white. This was before monofilament was used by fishermen. Only the rich or really dedicated anglers had rods and reels back in the early fifties. At any rate I was rigged differently than Dad and my older brothers with my black fishing line.

Dad got home from work that Friday and headed right into the bathroom to wash off a days work of coal dirt. If Dad ever came home clean, we all knew at first glance, Dad had not been in the mine. I do remember a few time that Dad would come home early carrying his round miners dinner bucket. When this happened I knew that Dad had not eaten his lunch, so I would run and greet him to get a sandwich or moon pie. Now that was a real fun thing, even if I was not hungry. This day he had completed his shift and was anxious to get cleaned up, so he could get all packed up and take his three sons over to Holston Lake.

The Tennessee Valley Authority had build a dam on the South Holston River and completed it in 1950. The work on the dam had been started in 1942, but during the war it was put aside for more important work. The work was resumed soon after WW II. The dam was 27 miles south of the Virginia-Tennessee line. This lake was still pretty new, and backed up several miles into Virginia. The fish had been stocked and were getting to be

Dahnmon's Little Stories

catching size. Of course the Holston River still had what ever fish it had, when it was dammed. News of great catches had abounded, and Dad was going to take us there.

Page 16

After Dad had his bath, Jerry and Larry had most of the stuff loaded up in Dad's 1950 Mercury. It was a neat car, only about two years old. It was a two door and painted black. It is the same car that Jerry got pulled over in, when Dad let him drive without a license, but that is another story.

We had the borrowed tent, old quilts, and blankets, cardboard boxes with produce from the garden, eggs, bread and whatever we had. Back then people didn't run to the store and buy everything for a trip like this. You ate whatever you had.

We motored over to the lake and arrived there in time to find a camp site and set up the tent. It was on a recline like an old road or maybe a planned boat ramp. Dad backed the 1950 Mercury down the hill to about twenty yards from the lake. This left plenty of room between the car and the water for our camp. The ground had been cleared, but there were stumps and rocks everywhere.

Jerry and Larry set up the tent, and the home made pegs worked just as well as the one's that came with the tent. They cleaned out most of the rough rocks and sticks where the tent was set up. I was mostly an observer, but my older brothers often called me lazy. I was watching and learning, I reckon. We got everything ready for the first night, lit a fire and Dad fried some potatoes. Not sure if we got any fishing in that evening or not, but I am sure we looked over the situation.

As darkness fell up on the little camp I was a

Dahnmon's Little Stories

little scared. We sat around the camp fire and talked for awhile before going to bed. I am sure that Dad was tired, he had been up since 5:00 AM, and worked all day in the coal mine before starting out with three boys.

We crawled back inside the little tent and wiggled out a place to sleep. After yakking for awhile we fell into slumber. It did not take too long to stay all night on Holston Lake. The Sun was getting up before I wanted to. Brother Jerry was digging under his blankets in search of something. Dad asked him what he was looking for.

"I slept on a rock or something and my back is killing me," Jerry answered.

Larry and I thought it was funny, but Dad told us it would not be funny if we were the ones sleeping on a rock.

After a breakfast of fried eggs and potatoes, we were ready for a big day of fishing. We were all anxious to try our luck angling. I was the one with the luck on this trip. It seemed every place we went on the big lake I caught a fish. Jerry and Larry took turns baiting my hook and taking fish off for me. They were happy to do it at first, but soon tired of the chore. I was cutting into their fishing time. They caught some fish, but even Dad was not having the luck I enjoyed.

Dad took us up to the end of the cove where the lake ended, and down the other side a little way to some stumps. Dad sat me down on a nice stump and we started fishing. Right off, the magic happened again. There was a school of young carp, I guess about a foot long each. They came to my bait like it was a magnet. I started yanking them out as fast as Jerry and Larry could take them off and re-bait my hook. They begin to complain profusely.

Dahnmon's Little Stories

"I can't even get my line in the water fore Dahnmon," said Larry.

"Me neither," Jerry added.

I caught a nice mess of fish, and Dad, Jerry, and Larry caught only a few. I thought it was really fun.

Later in the day Dad was talking to us about my great luck. He had thought it all out about why his little six year old son was catching all the fish. He reasoned that it had to be the fishing line. Remember that Dad, Jerry, and Larry all had new reed poles and white fishing lines. I had the little green sapling, but my fishing line was black. Near the end of our trip, Dad went and bought new line for the three of them. I think it was just fate, that I would be so lucky on my first overnight fishing trip. We ate the fish, even for breakfast.

That was a great trip for a man and his sons to bond and enjoy the great outdoors. I was only six, but so much of the details lodged into my memory bank. Jerry and Larry really had a good time too, but they would have liked it better if I shared more of the fish catching with them.

Dad was around thirty six at the time. This was an unusual trip, because Dad lived through the depression and would not miss a shift. As best I can remember we stayed three nights. It may have been on the week of the coal miner's vacation. Back then the mines would all shut down for a week each summer to allow them a vacation.

That time at the stump, I remember the fish to be Carp, Larry remembers them to be Bluegills, and Jerry remembers them to be Crappy. It is my story so I'm sticking with Carp.

Dad and my brothers helped me form some fond memories on that special trip. The next

Dahnmon's Little Stories

Summer I would be stricken with Meningitis and was almost taken to Heaven. God has been so good to me and I have enjoyed my life, especially fishing and hotdogs.

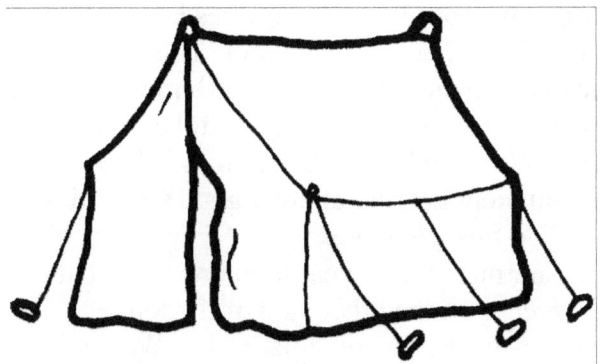

Dahnmon's Little Stories

A Tsunami On Straight Creek

While working in the Sheet Metal Trade, I ran the Heating, Ventilating, Air Conditioning work on the Ripley Ohio High School. This took place in 1991. This was a long drive from home so I and a couple of friends shared a camper and stayed right on the job site. We worked four ten hour days and headed home on Thursday evening each week.

There was some good fishing on Eagle Creek which empted into the Ohio River less than one half mile from the new school. This would be our pastime each evening after work. I brought my fourteen foot canoe, and kept it ready on the ladder rack of the little truck the company supplied me.

We started fishing just as soon as the weather warmed up enough, and fished almost every Monday, Tuesday, and Wednesday evening all summer long. Eagle Creek would rise and fall with the opening and closing of the Dam Locks down river on the Ohio, and stayed full a good mile up stream. We fished Eagle Creek most of the summer, but kept hearing about a good Creek down stream called Straight Creek.

Fishermen are like cattle in one way, The grass is greener on the other side of the fence, fishing is always better someplace else. We decided sometime in the near future we would travel to the other side of Ripley, and investigate the fishing possibilities on Straight Creek.

It was a hot muggy Wednesday afternoon about 5 PM when a thunder storm rolled in. The storm put a damper on our daily fishing. We went on to the camper, ate supper and cleaned up. The storm was just passing through and did not last very

Dahnmon's Little Stories

long. The Sun popped out with a blue sky, and this put us to thinking. It would be muddy around Eagle Creek, and we had already decided not to go fishing, but we could drive out and look at Straight Creek.

One of my friends, Jimmy wanted to wait by the phone; his wife was expecting a new baby any day. Jay the other friend suggested that we go and take a look at Straight Creek. Since I was curious about this new fishing possibility, I thought it was a good idea.

"Okay," I said, "we will just be looking, no need to take our fishing poles."

"Yes, lets take our poles and one lure, we might want to throw in a time or two," Jay answered.

We put our poles in the bed of the truck and drove down river a couple of miles to Straight Creek. Of course it was backed up because of the Ohio River Dam also. There was a nice marina set up with lots of boats. It looked like a lake. We followed the road around the deep water and started up the big hills that lay to the north of the Ohio River. We followed Straight Creek and it reminded me of some of the terrain in southwest Virginia and some of the trout streams I had fished. I guessed that we traveled about ten miles to a bridge that crossed the creek. We must have gained 500 feet in elevation since we left the road in Ripley.

We crossed the bridge and turned on to a dirt and gravel road that followed the creek down stream. I could not believe the beautiful mountain stream right here, this close to the Ohio River. The creek was clear as a crystal and very rocky.

Jay and I found a wide spot on the road and parked the truck. We walked over to look at the

Dahnmon's Little Stories

beautiful creek. It was shallow for the most part, with long areas of water three to four feet deep. There was not much sign that it had even stormed.

Between each long hole the water flowed fast like a mountain stream in Virginia. There were many large, mostly flat limestone rocks in the creek, and a limestone bottom. Sid and I got our fishing poles and found our way through the tall weeds and out on some of the rocks. The rocks were very slick.

"They should have named this Slippery Rock Creek," Jay said as he slipped along to another rock.

"You got that right!" I answered in agreement.

We started casting our baits out into the pools, and found that the creek was full of little Bass and Red Eyes. Most any place I tossed my artificial Crawdad a fish hit it. We caught something just about every time we cast out. I could not believe, in less than an hour ago the sky was black and we had heavy rains back at the camper.

I saw a shadow or two in the deeper water that might be a bigger fish, so I waded out into the pool with the four to five feet bank on my left. I carefully and quietly went up stream into the quiet pool. As I concentrated on my fishing I heard an unusual noise. It was a real loud noise, like the roar of a big truck, yet I couldn't recognize it. I looked around to my right and several feet back at Jay that was in the middle on one of his slick rocks. The noisy became increasingly louder.

"What is that noise?" I hollered at Jay.

"Could be a truck," he said concentrating on his fishing.

The noise now became a roar. I looked back to Jay again. His eyes were opened wide as he

Dahnmon's Little Stories

looked franticly up stream.

"Get the hell out of here!" he screamed and I turned back around to see what was going on up stream.

I could hardly comprehend what my eyes were telling me.

There was a wall of muddy water coming down the Creek that had to be 40 feet wide and ten feet tall. It was way up on each bank flattening the weeds, breaking down small trees and flipping large rocks like they were pieces of paper. The sound now sounded like a jet plane taking off, and here I stood in 3 feet of water. The bank on my left was at least head high and covered with big creek weeds. It was at least 30 feet back down the creek over the slippery bottom to where I came in.

A voice from within me spoke boldly, "Get up this bank now!"

I had the fishing pole in my hand and some how the crawdad plug hooked on to my shirt. I started to try to climb the steep bank, and got about a foot out of the water and slipped back into the water. I would have thrown away the fishing rod away, but the fishing plug was hanging in my shirt and pricking at my chest.

I heard the voice again just as plain as could be, "Get up the bank now!"

I'm not sure if it was God, my inner soul, or me saying it, but I think it was my Heavenly Father giving me fair warning.

I put my self in four wheel drive grabbed anything that was available and dug myself up the steep bank. Just as I cleared the bank I lunged forward in great strides to higher ground. Just as I reached safety I turned around to see the great wave go by.

COLONEL CHARLES DAHNMON WHITT

Dahnmon's Little Stories

Jay had beat me out of harms way by a few seconds and stood there hollering at me to hurry. He was in a much better place to evacuate the creek and avoid the danger.

I have heard of flash floods, some even take an hour to rise, but this was a Tsunami right here in Ohio. I have no doubt that God sent his Angel to save me that day.

Jay and I sat on the tailgate of the little truck to settle ourselves down. We could still find it hard to believe, what we had just witnessed. We were shook up the rest of the day. I prayed over and over thanking God for saving me that day.

When we got back to the camper, we could not come up with the words to fully describe what happened to Jimmy.

We were back at work the following Monday and decided to go back and look at Straight Creek. The tall creek weeds were flattened out, great flat rocks had been flipped, and brush was hanging in limbs as high as 10 feet above the ground. We noticed dead crawfish everywhere and the beautiful pools that once held so many fish were now void of any fish.

As we looked around, I couldn't help but look up the creek, afraid there might be another great wave of water to shun.

To this day I have never heard what caused the Tsunami on Straight Creek. Was there a dam that gave way, or was there a cloudburst up stream that caused such a flash flood?

God was not through with me, so he sent His Angel to rescue me on that faithful day!

Dahnmon's Little Stories

This is not the wave I saw, but it will give you an Idea of what a real flash flood looks like.

COLONEL CHARLES DAHNMON WHITT

Dahnmon's Little Stories

Working On The World Trade Center

It happened on the second Monday in March 1970. It was my sixth day working on the biggest job in the world.

Let me back up a little bit. I was living on Big Mountain Road about four miles out of Oliver Springs, Tennessee. I had been working about a year and a half out of old Local 51 Knoxville. Most of the last year had been on projects in and around the campus of the University of Tennessee. Work was becoming very scarce and we started having lay offs around Thanksgiving in 1969. The company I worked for did not like lying off folks, especially with Christmas coming up. None the less a few men got laid off every Friday. I was fortunate I and my partner Bob made it through Christmas, and about eight weeks more. It came down to only the boss, another foreman and his brother. There was not a sheet metal job that was not filled in Knoxville.

Bob and I had made a friend back in the summer. we worked with a man we called Yankee. He was a sheet metal journeyman out of local 28 New York, but formally of Knoxville. He had come down to work the summer and visit with family. After he was laid off he went back to New York City to work. He had told us to get in touch when we run out of work in Tennessee. It was time to call Yankee.

The trees were already putting out new leaves and flowers were blooming in sunny Tennessee. I hated the thought of heading off to New York. I figured it would be winter for at least another month that far north.

Bob made the phone call, and Yankee made

Dahnmon's Little Stories

arrangements with Danny Pascanuchi one of the Business Rep's with local 28. We started out early on a Sunday morning, and would drive to New York or close by and stay the night in a motel. We drove all day and found a little motel in New Jersey close to the George Washington Bridge. I had a fear of the unknown, how would I be treated, would I be able to do the job, what if the arrangements fell through and I didn't get hired? None the less we were up early and found the address of local 51 on a map. It was 351 Broadway and all we had to do was to cross the bridge a short distance to Broadway and drive south until we got there.

  I drove my 1968 Chevy pickup, which I called Big Orange Country. It was painted Orange, had a topper on the bed with Orange tinted windows. It also had the lettering on the back window which read, "Big Orange Country," in support of the University of Tennessee. Of course I took the name for my truck.

  We crossed the bridge that Monday and found we were in Yonkers, which I had never heard of, being off a dirt road in Tennessee. We found Broadway and I headed Big Orange south right into a heard of yellow taxies and New York commuters. I had never seen so much traffic in one place, in all my life.

  "Bob, you watch the building numbers and I will fight this traffic," I said.

  "Okay you get us down Broadway, and I will watch for 351," he answered.

  Honk, honk, honk, I don't think New Yorker's could drive with out their horns.

  "Pull in that lot, I think we are there," shouted Bob.

  I pulled Big Orange into the lot and parked,

Dahnmon's Little Stories

stepped out to find out that we were not at our destination. We got back into the truck and were ready to head out into the traffic again when a man ran up screaming at me.

"You owe seven dollar!" he said.

"What for?" I asked in an agitated manner?

"You parking here," he answered as one of the authorities of this land.

"I was here for one minute, you gonna charge for that?" I asked perplexed.

"Seven dollar!" he said again.

I begin to think that was the extent of his vocabulary.

"Don't pay him nothing," Bob hollered.

I stuck out a dollar to him and pulled out. The crazy man was still jumping up and down and he added several four letter words to his vocabulary by now.

Big Orange Country was making a few waves down Broadway again, and Bob was watching for the address again. We were getting close to southern Manhattan by now and Bob saw the Sheet Metal address. I saw another parking lot and headed into it.

Keep in mind that Big Orange Country is a short wheel base pickup.

A man came running out waving his arms, and hollering at me.

"We no take trucks here!" he said.

"Why, this truck ain't big as a sedan!" I proclaimed.

"We no take trucks!" he said affirmably.

We looked around and Bob spotted another parking lot just down the street.

I headed Big Orange to the next parking lot. I expected some funny talking fellow to come out

Dahnmon's Little Stories

waving his arms, but this guy was nice. We parked the truck and he gave us a ticket to reclaim Big Orange later. Sure enough we were looking at 351 Broadway. We got across the street by the grace of God, and climbed some stately steps to the Sheet Metal Local 28 office.

It had not been too great a day up to now, I did not know what to expect as we entered the big office.

We were treated graciously, and Danny Pascanuchi got us signed up to go to work. He told us to come with him and he would take us to the Job in his new 1970 Olds 98.

"What about our tools?" I asked.

"Don't worry you wouldn't need them today, my brother will get you settled in," Danny answered.

"Your brother?" Bob asked.

"Yes, my brother is the Steward for the job," he answered.

"Are we close to it?" Bob asked.

"About three blocks," Danny answered.

"What about my truck?" I asked.

"It will be just fine today, you can pick it up after work, and the Rebel will help you find a place to stay," Danny said.

"Rebel," I asked.

"I guess you know him by Yankee," Danny said laughingly.

"Danny, how big a job is this you are taking us to?" I asked.

"The biggest in the world," he answered.

Danny was very friendly to us misplaced Tennessee boys. We met the younger Pascanuchi, and he got us settled in on the job. We met our new foreman, and many of the guys. Yankee came down

Dahnmon's Little Stories

to greet us and make plans to help us get a room. He had already been looking over on Staten Island. He had an apartment over there.

The day went fast as they only worked a seven hour day in 1970. After we got off we headed for the parking lot where I left Big Orange for the day. They made me pay $15.00 which was a big deal in 1970.

Yankee headed for Staten Island with Big Orange glued to his bumper. We crossed the big bridge (Verrazano-Narrows) from Brooklyn over to Staten Island. This was the longest suspension bridge in the world until 1980.

Bob and I found a room to rent in a private home, and settled in. This house was a three story house with a story of its own. The folks were Italian and the men wore double breasted suites when they came to see their aged mother every Sunday. Big Orange was completely safe from thief's and vandal's while parked at this house.

Every day we would drive about three miles, park on the street near the Staten Island Ferry station. We would ride the big yellow boats across the bay and walk about three blocks to the Twin Tower job site.

Now back to my story about that sixth day at work on the World Trade Center. I had heard all the week before about one of the Kangaroo Cranes dropping a piece of steel and it went through six floors before it stopped on the seventh. I had this in the back of my mind as I went about my work.

The Kangaroo Cranes were set up to cover each corner. There was four cranes on each tower and could be jacked up as the building progressed. I heard that the cranes were imported from Austral. They could handle huge loads. I asked around "how

Dahnmon's Little Stories

will they ever get them down from 110 stories up?"

Some of the other workers explained that one crane would let the other three down and the last one would be unassembled and taken down in a large cargo elevator, a piece at a time. The cranes were a source of conversation.

I could see structural steel rising by the edge of the building as I worked. The cable was really long and thick. Some of the steel was marked, showing its weight to be fifty tons or more.

We always worked at least seven floors under the concrete pours as a safety measure. The concrete would be pumped to the floor just under the last decking that had been set.

The job was so big, that they added communication speakers on each floor as the concrete hardened enough to get on it. This way the workers could send messages and get instructions from whomever. Of course they had a Yankee speaking New Yorker as the mediator. After about five days I was beginning to understand the foreign New York English. The people loved to hear me talk, so I had plenty of visitors each day, even my superintendent.

The second Monday at work I was on the 18th floor going about my business installing duct work. I heard an enormous blast that shook the building. My first thought was, which way do I run? I thought another missile of steel was making its way through the floors. As I stood there frozen in my tracks, not knowing which way to run, I heard the voice of the New Yorker on the speaker.

Another blast hit the building as I ran to the speaker. I looked around and did not see anyone on the 18th floor.

Dahnmon's Little Stories

The New Yorker was speaking in a frantic tone, "Evacuate the building!" He said it over and over. I ran to the temporary elevator and that sucker was gone. I heard another blast which put me into a more desperate mode. The only option I had was to run down the eighteen flights of stairs. As another blast hit, I hurried even faster thinking, what have I got myself into and will I get out of this alive?

Eighteen flights of stairs seemed endless during this trip to the ground. By the time I got on the ground the building had been shaken seven times. It was soon revealed to me, the cause of all of this commotion.

It was still cold weather this time of year in New York City, so the contractors had made fire places by cutting steel barrels in half and adding a grate. They had coal brought to the job and each crew took coal to their place of work each morning.

There were buildings coming out of the ground all around the Twin Towers, and one of these about two stories down below ground level were the source of the trouble. Iron workers, "Iron Heads", us "Tin Knocker's" called them, had set up one of these fire place's right in front of seven acetylene bottles. The situation was a bomb waiting to go off, and it did, seven times. I have never understood why they went off one at a time, I thought that they should have all went off with the first, but we were spared a blast seven times bigger by the way it happened. The blast blew out the glass windows in the second story to about the fifth story in all the surrounding buildings. No one was hurt other than scratches, and the shock of the blasts. If they all blew at once it is hard to say what the damage might have been. I was really relieved that it was not the whole building falling down around

Dahnmon's Little Stories

me.

Our superintendent made phone's accessible to all of us "Traveler's" so we could call home. He was afraid that it would be on national news and the home folks would be in a panic.

I got over this day and worked about five and a half more months on this great building. I saw many things while working on this job. From fires, a man fell to his death from the 25th floor, I saw police pulling out bodies from the East River, I worked above the clouds many days, and went to the ground several times because of bomb threats being called in. I saw ocean cruisers, and I saw the great Statue of Liberty, waving to all that enter New York Harbor. I saw Ironworkers throwing connecting bolts down several stories on the hippies trying to tear down the United States flag. I marched down Broadway with hundred's of construction workers and the girls from all the offices, in support on Nixon sending troops into Cambodia. This was my exciting adventure as a young man out in the world in 1970.

I cried on 9/11/2001 when these great buildings fell!

Dahnmon's Little Stories

The grand "Twin Tours" also know as the World Trade Center. They fell to terrorist on September 11, 2001.

COLONEL CHARLES DAHNMON WHITT

Dahnmon's Little Stories

Inside A Jet Plane, Didn't know If I'd Get Out Again!

While serving in the United States Navy, at Oceania Naval Air Station in the summer of 1966 I went through an ordeal. This was a Master Jet Base in Virginia Beach Virginia serving the fleet during the Viet Nam War. The squadrons of fighters and attack aircraft were based here while the Aircraft Carriers were in home port at Norfolk Naval Base.

I was part of what we called Ship's Company, and we had about twelve aircraft assigned to us to maintain and we also took care of transient aircraft coming in with problems. We called these problems "Gripes"!

The summer of 1966, I was an Aviation Structural Mechanic 3rd class. I was of the sheet metal type which dealt mostly with an aircraft's body (fuselage), air controls, and the like. There were two other types of Aviation Structural mechanic's, these were hydraulics, and safety equipment such as ejection seats. We all intermingled as needed. All three types had a basic idea about the others. I happened to be on duty this summer day, when a Navy F-9 from another base, landed with a hydraulic gripe.

The pilot announced he was loosing hydraulic fluid somehow, and he wanted it fixed ASAP, so he could get airborne again. Chief Hewlett the line chief had a quick fix which alarmed the pilot and me as I would be involved.

Normally we would pull an aircraft into the hanger, set it up on jacks, and hook up a Hydraulic

Dahnmon's Little Stories

Jenny. (Pump) This way the controls could be worked and any leaks would become obvious. This was the correct way to deal with such problems.

The Pilot was in a hurry, and Chief Hewlett would accommodate him by taking unnecessary risks. Now I must say the Chief had been around and had seen this done before, but that did not seem like the right thing to do. His plan was for me to be inside the air intake and to watch for the leak as the pilot fired up the screaming jet engine.

The pilot looked intently at the Chief.

"Chief, are you sure about this?" asked the pilot.

"Sure, Yes Sir," replied Chief Hewlett.

"I have seen this done several times on the old F-9," he confirmed.

Chief Hewlett explained to the pilot that I would not be harmed, the turbine blades on this model of aircraft were encased with hardware cloth, (rat wire) and the worst thing that could happen was that I would be sucked up against the wire.

Chief Hewlett had me empty my pockets of anything that could fly into the engine. He had a rope brought out, and had me tie it around my ankle, and gave me a pair of Mickey Mouse Ears (hearing protection head set), and asked the pilot to get in the plane and fire it up once I was inside the intake. He explained that the cam shell doors would open once the engine was running and give me light to see the leak.

The pilot looked at me standing by the intake with the rope tied to my leg and another sailor (Airman George Trump) holding the other end. He looked back at Chief Hewlett.

"Chief, are you sure about this?" he asked again.

COLONEL CHARLES DAHNMON WHITT

Dahnmon's Little Stories

"It will be just fine, Petty Officer Whitt will see the leak and we can get it fixed quickly," he said.

The stage was set, and the only one sure about things was the Chief. I was not too sure about it, who ever heard of a man being in the intake of a jet plane while the engine was being fired up.

The pilot climbed into the cockpit and readied himself to fire the engine. Chief Hewlett nodded for me to crawl inside the intake. The sailor holding the rope stood to the side of the intake and fed the rope as I crawled to the very back of the metal tunnel, next to the engine. I must say I was having scary thoughts, being back inside the bowels of a war plane in the darkness and feeling the closeness of the tight space.

The Chief signaled the pilot to fire the engine. He fired it up and ran it up to a high RPM, before backing off to a steady run as they usually did.

The noise was horrific, and the wind coming by me rolled up my bell bottom dungarees plumb past my knees. It took all I had not to panic. The cam shell doors on top of the fuselage cracked open because of the lack of air to the great engine. I composed myself for an instant and looked around for a leak. There it was and I took a mental picture. I was done, get me out of this thing I signaled by trashing both legs against the inside of the tight intake.

The Chief signaled the pilot to shut it down and Airman Trump holding the rope began to pull me out. As I bent my body to allow my feet to touch the deck the Chief was laughing at the sight. My britches were rolled up past my knees, and my shirt was up around my neck The chief saw my face and

Dahnmon's Little Stories

quit laughing.

"Did you find the leak?" Chief Hewlett asked.

"Yes I know where it is," I answered.

I patiently put myself back together, and untied the rope on my leg. Chief Hewlett and I got up on the wing and pushed down on the cam shell door. I pointed to the leak and jumped down off the F-9. The Chief showed the other sailor and he reached in and with his wrench tightened up the loose fitting. He next checked the reservoir and added fluid.

By now the pilot was on the deck and came over and personally thanked me for doing what I did. I acted brave, but it scared the stuffing's out of me. I decided that day that I would never do such a stunt again, no matter who ordered it.

The pilot got back into his bird, and the crew sent him toward the runway. He gave me a wave, and I gave him a salute as he parted.

So you see I was inside a jet plane, and didn't know if I would get out again. The more modern jets around the base would have chewed me up, and spit me out as burnt hamburger. I suggest you never try this at home.

Dahnmon's Little Stories 56

This is the type of jet (F-9) that I went into the intake!

Helping Big Brother With His
COLONEL CHARLES DAHNMON 56
WHITT

Dahnmon's Little Stories

Paper Route

I was about 8 or 9 I think when Larry my big brother first called on me to help with his paper route. He would only call on me if he was running late or in a hurry for some reason.

Larry, about 13, had a big route that covered several miles, and he did it all on his trusty bike. He was up early each morning and headed up the dirt road we lived on in Stinson Bottom. It was up hill about a quarter of a mile to the Old White Church, where they dropped off his papers each morning. After spending time rolling up the papers and placing them in the two bags, he would coast down the hill into West Raven and deliver all of them. Next he would climb the hill by the Church again and coast down the east side into the little town of Raven. He worked his way through backside of the little town and into Red Ash a little coal camp. He delivered to all of the customers in Red Ash Hollow and up another big hill to the main road, Route U.S. 460. He delivered to that area and coasted down the big hill probably gaining a speed of forty miles an hour back into the front part of Raven. Next he would cover the lower end of Doran. Then he would transverse Raven Hill back to the old Raven Church where he had started. It was down hill from there and he had customers down the hill and more around the circle of homes on the two dirt roads off the main dirt road. (About two blocks) and he was home and had to get ready for school.

I remember the first time he called on me to help. He got me awake and helped me to get dressed. I was not too enthused about the idea. It would be dark out there and I was afraid of the dark.

Dahnmon's Little Stories

I was always afraid of the dark and many other things. Mom said it was due to my bout with rheumatic fever. All I know is that I was afraid.

We were raised in a Christian home and I knew about God and all of his power, but I also knew it was scary out on these country roads with not a sign of a street light. I had even heard of Ghosts playing around the old White Church during the dark hours.

I stuck close to Larry and helped him roll his papers, and my job was to go back down into Stinson Bottom and take care of our neighbor customers. I didn't want to leave the security of my big brother, and head out into the darkness even though I had a flash light.

Larry told me something that morning that has stuck with me for over fifty years.

"Dahnmon, God will protect you when you pray and ask him to. It will even help to sing out loud, "God Will Protect Me," Larry explained.

Finally Larry headed down into West Raven and I headed down into Stinson Bottom singing about as loud as I could, "God will protect me!"

I felt the calmness of God that morning in my young life, and I still pray for his protection.

It must have been some sight, the little boy flashing his light back and forth and singing as loud as possible, "God will protect me!"

I owe a lot to my Brothers, Mom, Dad and Almighty God!

Dahnmon's Little Stories

This is not Jerry or Larry, but it fits the times!

Dahnmon's Little Stories

Nails And Boards

At an early age I found that I loved tools and making things! I guess this is what led to my vocation as a Sheet Metal Worker. Dad noticed that I had interest in hand tools and he (Santa) encouraged me by giving me a little tool set one Christmas. It was not a toy tool set, but a functional set on a smaller scale. The hammer was small as well as the hand saw. They were real tools that Dad would borrow when he wanted to do a little job. He would just grab out a tool, rather than going out to the smoke house to get his! I was pleased that Dad would use my tools; this made me know that they were real McCoy's! Of course I used Dads hammer and saws, I think that is one reason Santa brought me my own tools that Christmas.

I became quiet proficient at driving nails, a friend Kenny, and I would build tree houses and other club houses! We would go up and down Mill Creek and salvage the boards that high water would bring us! God had put some tall ash trees on the upper end of my empire. (Dad's Lot) Kenny and I would nail boards of about two feet long up the trees to create a ladder. We would get way up in the tree to the first big forks and build our fort there. Kenny was a little older and bigger than me, so he would pull up the boards I tied on the rope. It is a wonder we are here today! We never fell, but a board came untied as Kenny was pulling it up one day. The board was light because it was rotten. It fell across my head and broke.

As I staggered around, Kenny yelled down at me!

"You all right?" he asked.

COLONEL CHARLES DAHNMON WHITT

Dahnmon's Little Stories

I whimpered out a little whine.

Kenny saw that I was alright, and said, "Damn, your head is harder than that board!"

I didn't see the humor in it!

One of my projects was a new club house built on the ground. It was in a flood plain so I built it on stilts! I knew when the spring rains came Mill Creek would back up from the flooded Clinch River.

I was really pleased with my accomplishment, until my big brother saw it. He laughing said, "It looks like a toilet!"

Another project I had was to convert my 4 Radio Flyer wagon wheels into a wooden down hill racer! I used my imagination and added a steering wheel and hand brake! It was a fun thing to fly down the old gravel road on church house hill, pretending I was in a great race!

As I said, I got good at driving nails, and I used up Dad's nails about as fast as he would buy them. I can still hear him fussing when he would look for a nail to repair something!

"That young-un gets every nail I bring in," Dad would say.

Yet I don't think he minded too much. He never ever said leave my stuff alone. He kept his tools and nails out in an oak board building that was once used as a smoke house. Those boards were as hard as steel!

I went to the Richlands Fair one year, and saw a way to get a Teddy Bear at one of the gambling joints. They had a 4 X 4 set up like a saw horse. They started 3 two inch nails in the board. You would put up a Quarter (25 cents) and try to drive all the nails into the board with three hits of the hammer. I noticed that they started the nails on an angle to make you bend the nails while striking them.

I plopped down my quarter and took the hammer. I aimed the hammer on the exact angle and gave each nail a strong blow. Bam, Bam, Bam, the nails all three were driven down to the head in the 4 X 4.

The woman gave me a big Teddy Bear! Her boss hurried over to her, and started instructing her as to how to start the nails.

"I did start them on an angle," she said, "That kid can drive nails!"

I walked away with my trophy, knowing I could have cleaned them out of Teddy Bears!

Dahnmon's Little Stories 63

COLONEL CHARLES DAHNMON 63
WHITT

Dahnmon's Little Stories

A New Year!

We all get to start over as a new year comes to town! Some face it with a smile; some face it with a frown.

Up north is very cold, but down south it is pleasant and warm! Some treat it with love, some look on it as harm!

We all know the past, and some of it was not fun! We are in the Present, which often gives us alarm!

We look to the future with glee! We all hope it has the Key!

No matter how old we get, we remember the past as if happened yesterday! We don't know what to do in the Present day! Now we can start over and hope for a new day!

What is our hope? What is our prayer? Should we talk about it, or will we jinx whatever is there?

Our life is like the leaves on a tree! We start out little and green! We grow up and experience the warm summer breeze!

As our life rolls on we run out of time, we look to the past, and remember the great times!

As we get older we tire and wrinkle up! Looks like the future is gone, we may as well give up!

But let's not give up as we fall to the ground, our lives will give hope to the new little green ones!

God calls us to live and to help the ones on the ground! God is our hope and leads us along!

So this New Years Day, lets contemplate, stop and pray! The Good Lord has given us another day!

COLONEL CHARLES DAHNMON WHITT

Dahnmon's Little Stories

What Price?

What "Price" will you give? Don't worry it's free!

Is there really a Heaven? Is there really a Hell?

God wrote the word, it is for us to read!

If God wrote the word, it is for us to read!

If God wrote the word, it is for us to heed!

Yes there is a Heaven, the price has been paid!

Yes there is a Hell! For those that don't heed, their fate is made!

So remember with Jesus the price has been paid!

So remember with Satan our fate is made!

Dahnmon's Little Stories

Jesus arose and so will we!

COLONEL CHARLES DAHNMON WHITT

Dahnmon's Little Stories

The Scare on High Knob

While camping with my Scout Troop at the park on High Knob Mountain near Coeburn Virginia, It rained like a Monsoon. After a day and two nights of staying in leaky Pup Tents, our Scout Master W.W. Smith had enough! He went to a phone to call a friend that had a Hunters Cabin on out the Mountain in some of the most Primitive land east of the Mississippi River. The man told W. W. Smith that he was welcome to take the troop to the cabin, and relayed the location of the hidden key.

We broke camp that wet morning, loaded up our wet stuff and headed out for another new adventure. Back in these days deer and other game was scarce, but not on High Knob. Most of us had never seen a deer out in the wild before. As we traveled out the little mountain road we counted over twenty deer as we passed.

Guess what, the rain stopped as we came up on the little cabin. As we got out of the little bus, the first thing we saw in the soft ground was, Bear Tracks! Wow!, this sent fear abounding into every boy there, and probably our Scout Master too! Of course he tried to calm our souls by telling us that a bear would not bother a bunch of noisy boys. This did not help us too much!

We moved into the cabin with all out gear. There was about a dozen of us. We only had enough floor space for all the boys to lie down.

There was no water or plumbing, so Rev. W.W.Smith (Scoutmaster) told me and Frankie to stay at the cabin and watch our stuff, while he took all the other boys on an expedition to look for drinking water.

Dahnmon's Little Stories

After all the boys left Frankie and I were quiet scared there by ourselves. We were both church goers and I had a little Bible in my gear. I don't remember how I knew about the 91st Psalms, but I turned there and begin to read God's word!

The 91st Psalm is all about how God gives his followers protection. This was soothing to our souls, in a time of distress. After reading the word Frankie and I had a little prayer meeting up on the mountain sitting there in that little cabin. We were still alert, but were not so scared after our talk with God.

It wasn't long before we heard a commotion as all the boys came running back to the cabin. They had had a frightful encounter with a large Black Bear out in the woods.

They gave us a report that they came up on him and he lowered his head and extended his neck while letting out a loud growl. The bruin never offered to back up or run. This was his mountain and he would defend it if it came to that. The boys panicked and ran in different directions all leading to the shelter of the Hunter's Cabin! W.W. Smith tried not to show alarm, but was on the heels of the running scouts.

We all decided we did not want to build a fire outside of the cabin to cook our suppers. So we all sit in the cabin eating various canned foods cold and right out of the cans. I never will forget I opened a can of spaghetti, dumped it into my surplus mess kit which had some spilled soap powders in it. I never noticed the soap until I begin to eat. I ate around the soap the best I could.

Our Scout Master tried to act brave and even said he was going to put his sardine can out side the door to attract the bear. He was always fooling with

Dahnmon's Little Stories

us like that. I did notice he stayed in the cabin with the rest of us.

We had a restless night and when we got up to go out side for latrine purposes, the first thing we saw was fresh bear tracks that led to the cabin! That insolent bruin had followed the running scouts right to the cabin! Needless to say we were alert that morning.

Our Scout Master decided to move us one more time. He knew about a church camp over in Lee County, Virginia that was open and not too far away. We never let on about being scared, but none complained about packing up and heading off the mountain and wilds of High Knob.

This was just another time in my young life that I called upon the God of Creation in a time of trouble and fear.

Dahnmon's Little Stories

How Did I Get Here?

How did I get here, let me see!

I started out as a baby on my mama's knee!

I ate like a pig and grew real keen!

I went to school, looked around and said; how did I get here?

Shut up, sit down, learn that spelling and math; Oh my goodness, my head is full and a spinning!

I looked around again; how did I get here?

I went to high school, but didn't quite fit in!

I took my classes but did not do well! How did I get here?

I took up football, but I was too small and slow as a snail; coach said keep my head up, but all I got was a blooded nose. How did I get here?

I met a Navy Man, he told me he had a plan for me; I took the test that all thought I would flunk! I aced that sucker and was promised the world, or was it see the world?

They flew me to boot camp, I felt just fine! Next thing I knew I was cussed down to the ground! How did I get here?

COLONEL CHARLES DAHNMON WHITT

Dahnmon's Little Stories

I did real well; they said I was swell, could I sign up for another tour?

"No" I said, "you got me once!" I ran and checked out and got out of that place!

I was so pleased; how did I get here?

I met a woman; I thought she was sweet as honey! She departed for another! How did I get here?
I worked for the man, never had a plan, how will I get out of here? Will I ever retire; I doubt I will ever make it! How did I get here?

I met another woman, this one is for me! How did I get here?

I met my Lord Jesus and He really had a plan! How did I get here?

Finally I died and went to this beautiful place! No crying, no pain, just walking around Heaven all day! How did I get here? I know now, It was the Lord Jesus who saved me!

Dahnmon's Little Stories   72

Jesus took my place on the cross!

He is our Advocate with The Father

**COLONEL CHARLES DAHNMON   72
WHITT**

Dahnmon's Little Stories

What Is A Creek?

What is a creek, it is Heaven sent! It is a joy to see and refreshing for a boy to play in!

A creek is like a river but God made it small! It was just right for a boy like me!

My Mommy said stay away from there, you will get hurt, but it drew me like a magnet!

The creek had minnows, those delightful little fish! It had crawdads that looked like little lobsters!

It had big tree roots that stuck out into the water, watch out here for the scary wiggling snake!

It had tall weeds that grew along it's banks, Oh! What a delightful place!

I learned so much about life while just playing along the creek!

It had ducks, and under it's banks It had muskrats too!

I caught my first fish, even though it was small, It meant so much to a boy like me!

It did have some traps I soon learned about; the three leafed Poison Ivy was waiting for me!

COLONEL CHARLES DAHNMON WHITT

Dahnmon's Little Stories

When I think of my life and all that I have been through, It was that little creek that prepared me so well! It had training, and comfort too!

I fell through its ice and was really cold! I found that the world was much like this too, if you skate on thin ice you will fall in!

It was refreshing in summer to splash and play, I have never found anything better in this world!

God made my creek, it was just right for a boy like me!

Dahnmon's Little Stories

A boy and his creek!

Dahnmon's Little Stories

My Motel Adventures

Working as a Sheet Metal Worker in the construction field, I spent many nights in motels. Some were nice others not so nice, I picked what my expense account could provide. Some funny things happened and of course some things that scared me somewhat.

I was staying at a motel in Athens, Ohio one summer by myself. I had been knocking holes for future ductwork and was really tired. After eating out I settled into the bed and watched a show or two on the television. I finally decided I was ready to go to sleep so I turned off the lights and television. All was quiet for awhile, when all of a sudden the television came on by itself startling me. It was loud and bright as I had been almost asleep. I got up and turned it off with the power button, settled down again for a nights sleep. Bam, it did it again, and scared me once more. I got up and unplugged it. I made up my mind if that thing came on one more time I was out of there!

Another time I was staying in a pretty nice motel in Covington, Kentucky and working across the river in Cincinnati. After I got to bed and was almost asleep, I heard a knock on my door. Being cautious I ask who it was and a man's slurred voice sounded back an answer.

"Let me in Bill, I want to borrow a dollar," the voice said.

"Go away, ain't no Bill in here," I answered.

"Come on Bill, I know you are in there," he answered.

By now I realized I was talking to a drunk or crazy person. I told him one more time that there

Dahnmon's Little Stories

was no Bill there.

"Come on Bill, let me borrow a dollar, you ain't fooling me," the voice came through the thin door once again.

Anger rose up in me and I wanted to open that door and sucker punch that fool! But I controlled myself and went to the phone and called the motel office and reported it to them. They explained that the fellow was going all over the motel trying to find Bill and that security would take him away from my door. I am thankful I didn't follow my angry inclinations and hit the drunk. He most likely would have gone over the second floor banister to the ground. I finally got back to sleep.

At least three times I have checked into rooms and the desk clerk gave another guest a key to my room. Here I sat in my underwear and someone starts opening my door. This is also unnerving. I had learned to always fasten the night chain or latch after the first time.

Another thing happened in southern Columbus at a motel. I had settled in and had watched the television for awhile. I turned off the light about 10:10 PM. After another minute or two passed my phone rang. I reached over got the phone, turned on the light and answered.

"Hello, are you Billy Whitt, working at so and so?" asked a hefty voice.

"No, I am Charlie Whitt, I work for Columbus Furnace, you have the wrong number," I said.

I hung up the phone turned off the light and lay back down to unwind.

The crazy phone rang again. I turned on the light and answered the phone again.

"Mister Wheat, if you don't know dis man,

Dahnmon's Little Stories

don't open the door," said the little Indian desk clerk.

What now, I wondered.

Bam, Bam, Bam, went the hard knocks on the door. It sounded like this guy was ten feet tall and the door could crash down anytime!

"Who are you and what do you want?" I screamed.

Bam, Bam, Bam sounded the knocks again.

"Open the door," sounded the giant of a man that only a little thin a door separated us.

My mind was racing as I tried to figure out what was going on. My first thought was this guy has me mixed up with someone courting his wife.

Bam, Bam, Bam, went the knocks; I rolled off to the floor between the two beds, grabbed the phone and punched "0" for the front desk. The nervous Indian on duty answered.

"Call the cop, this guy is going to break down the door," I screamed into the phone.

"I call cops," answered the little Indian.

I usually carry my 45 automatic pistol on trips like this, but thank God I didn't have it this time. I may have shot through the door, but all I could do was lay there and wait.

The phone rang once again; I reached up on the night stand and grabbed it.

"Cops come," said the little Indian clerk.

A funny thing happened next. The gruff voice out side my door hollered at me saying, "You might as well come out, the cops are coming!"

Why would he say that, the cops are coming to get him, not me I thought?

After a minute or two the man left my door. And in another five minutes a quiet knock was heard at my door. I sneaked over and pull back the

Dahnmon's Little Stories

curtain a bit to gander out. It was two police officers wearing their blue uniforms. I opened the door and politely said, "Glad to see you fellers, some big guy was trying to knock down my door," I exclaimed.

"Can we come in?" ask the closest police officer.

"Sure, come on in," I answered.

They walked in and looked all around.

"May we look in the bathroom," one asked.

"Go ahead," I answered wondering what on earth was going on.

After they were satisfied that there were no one else in the room, they were ready to leave.

"Do you know who that guy was knocking at my door?" I asked.

The policeman smiled and said, "Bounty Hunter, looking for a Billy Whitt."

"You mean they still have Bounty Hunters?" I asked.

"Good thing you didn't open your door Mister Whitt, he would have beat you up and then ask questions, replied the policeman.
I never got much sleep that night, and was cautious going out the door the next morning.

Another time I was working in Athens, Ohio and staying in a motel. It had been a trying and tiring week. I usually worked four ten hour days and headed home on Thursday evening. I was familiar with the motel room because I had stayed there for several weeks. At any rate I headed home and drove eighty some miles to my home.

After a good supper and bath I was ready to go to bed. My wife Sharon and I retired for the night and I quickly fell asleep. Then it happened. I awaken about half way. I was tired and thought I was in the motel room. I looked at my wife's long

Dahnmon's Little Stories

black hair in the darkness and thought there had been a large BEAVER in bed with me. It was scary to say the least. How on earth could a beaver get into my room and even in my bed? I cautiously reached over to touch the beaver to see if it was real. I touched it and of course it was my wife's hair. Sharon moved at my touch and I let out a scream and jumped clean out of bed. This scared my wife and she screamed. Sharon rose up and looked at me standing there in my skivvies.

"What on earth are you doing?" she asked.

"I thought your hair was a beaver in bed with me," I said sheepishly.

She laughed out loud at my sight and story. After I was satisfied her hair was not a big old beaver I was ready to get back to sleep. We have had several laughs about this happening over the years.

Dahnmon's Little Stories

Young Aviation

As I grew up in the hills of southwest Virginia, I learned many things from my big brothers. One of these was the art of building and flying kites. Every year when March came in, the wind came with it. That brought out the kite flyers. I remember that Jerry and Larry would let out so much line that there kite would appear as a tiny dot dancing in the wind way above the McGlothlin Ridge we flew on. They flew way across the Clinch River bottom.

One evening Jerry was flying his kite way out, when suppertime came. Mommy went out and hollered for him to come and eat. Jerry had a dilemma, how could he wind in his kite and hurry off the ridge and get to the house for supper? When Mommy hollered, you listened and you ran home! Jerry started winding it in and realized that it would take some-time. Back then folks sat down to eat as a family not as come and go like today. Jerry knew he had to cut the line, or come up with a good commonsense answer.

Jerry looked over the situation and saw a lone fence post a few yards away. He simply walked over and tied his kite string to the post and scooted down the ridge to supper. Jerry told everyone at the table that his kite was flying itself with the help of a fence post. This brought some smiles and even a laugh. Someone said that thing would be on the ground before he could do his chores and get back to the kite. I am not sure, but maybe Jerry didn't have to wash dishes that day, but I remember he got back up on the ridge and casually wound in the kite.

Jerry and Larry built their own kites most of

Dahnmon's Little Stories

the times and repaired them as needed. They would use the paper from the drycleaners. Back then plastic was not in wide use. The light paper, tan in color made good kite material. The only thing it lacked the bright colors of the store bought kites. I also made a few kites as I learned the skill from my older brothers.

Some other things I learned was the way to wind in a kite and to add a tail for high wind usage. My brothers had learned a method to expedite bringing the kite in. They would wind the kite string the normal way until they got a ball started in the middle of their stick. The stick was about an inch in diameter and six to eight inches long. After they got a nice ball in the middle they would wind end over end crossing the ball which brought string in faster. As for tails, they would use light weight rags and tie them at the bottom of the kite to keep it from nose diving. It was experimental as to how much tail you used on a given day according to the amount of wind.

I bought myself a box kite one March. To this day I don't understand how they fly, but they fly nicely. They can become boring after awhile just setting up there riding the wind. I have not seen a box kite in many years; someone should put them back on the market.

As I got older I became interested in model airplanes, the ones with the little engines. I got my first one for Christmas. It was plastic and had short lines to fly it with. It was more of a learning experience than anything else.

The way you controlled them was quiet simple. The elevator on the back of the model planes moved up and down just like the real ones. You had a handle with two lines attached. You held

Dahnmon's Little Stories

the handle vertical as you flew the planes. The lines went into the left wing and into the fuselage to a turn-tee. From there two lines went back to the elevator. As you angle the handle back the elevator rose thus the model plane rose and if you angled the handle down the plane went down. The rudder was fixed in place, turned to the right thus causing the model plane to try and fly away from you and keeping the lines tight.

As I learned about this fun hobby, I moved up to building much larger planes from balsa wood and silk-span. After buying the kit you would assemble the plane by gluing the wood pieces together and cover with the silk-span. Next you would paint the silk-span with model plane dope, a clear substance about the same as clear fingernail polish. As the dope dried the silk-span shrink up to a strong tight skin. Then you could add color paint to your own taste.

The planes according to size would require different size engines. I remember I got my dream engine, a McCoy 35; it would deliver six tenths of horsepower and sounded like a screaming demon. I began to think that anything would fly if you put a McCoy 35 on it.

I had many crashes and learned to repair the planes. This developed into a new design of my own. I built a flying wing and it flew. It was heavy and bulky which made it slower than most of the model planes.

I got pretty good at flying my planes and would have dog fights with my friends. We would both stand together in the flying circle and have two of our friends start the engines and launch them together. We added about three feet of crepe paper one inch wide to the tails. As we chased each other

Dahnmon's Little Stories

we would cut off the paper of each others plane with the spinning propellers.

I got a good background in aviation by building and flying these little planes on 50 feet of thin steel cable. I once was flying as a thunder storm was approaching and the air became filled with static electricity. The charge shot up the little cables and was jolting me pretty good. I wanted to turn loose but I knew my plane would crash. I held on dancing around until the fuel ran out and I landed my plane.

As I stated I got a good background in aviation and when I joined the U.S. Navy I put this information on my application for school and was sent to naval aviation school to be an Aviation Structural Mechanic. A few times while in service I repaired the fabric tears on the old Beech Craft C-45 and C-47 elevators just like I did on the little model planes. The only difference was that you sewed the tear with a baseball stitch and placed a piece of fabric over the tear and put the dope to it.

While serving in the Navy I got to fly often up and down the east coast from Florida to Rhode Island as an air crewman. My hobbies as a young person paid off as I put it to use in the U.S. Navy.

Dahnmon's Little Stories

COLONEL CHARLES DAHNMON WHITT

Dahnmon's Little Stories

What The Flag Means To Me

Many years ago our forefathers sought freedom from an overbearing king!

Give liberty or give me death!

The patriots needed a flag to carry and represent them, Betsy Ross stepped up.
Betsy's flag of thirteen would be tested greatly!

Another flag flew with the ragged Stars and Strips; the blue flag of the French.

The tattered Stars and Stripes prevailed against the most powerful country in the world, because "In God We Trust."

Our banner was attacked again by the same great nation in 1812. Once again God was with us.

Our National Anthem was written by Francis Scott Key as he watched the bombardment at Baltimore.

All night long bombs burst in air.

God was there and with the dawn the flag was still there.

Then we had a war within our self and God cried.

The Stars and Bars of the south blew

COLONEL CHARLES DAHNMON WHITT

Dahnmon's Little Stories

mightily against Old Glory. Both sides thought God was with them, but God taught us a lesson and gave freedom to many.

Old Glory would go to a World War and help preserve freedom to others again. This time she would repay France for her help in the past, and freedom rang.

The German Cross blew hard against Old Glory and the Rising Sun dived into our ships, but God was with us.

Had God not helped Old Glory, we might be speaking German today.

To me our flag represents God given Freedom!

Dahnmon's Little Stories

COLONEL CHARLES DAHNMON WHITT

Dahnmon's Little Stories

SON OF A COAL MINER

My Daddy was a Coal Miner!

If he came home early with a clean face, I knew he had a treat for me.

I would run to meet him so I could get the goodies from his round dinner bucket.

He would have a ballony sandwich and maybe some fruit. If I was lucky there would be a little cake too.

I did not know the trouble and dangers Daddy went through for me.

He would come home with a black face of love; it had to be given to him from God above.

He was surely a man of God and had many Guardian Angels.

One day the angles were surely busy protecting other miners and a great rock fell on my Daddy.

He prayed and talked to the men trying to make him free.

He did not faint away and he told them what to do. They shored up the roof, but the rock was too big to move.

Daddy was on a Motor* so he rocked himself free.   * A battery powered flat vehicle used by mine foreman.

Dahnmon's Little Stories

They put Daddy in a rough riding truck; on across the rough road they went with their precious cargo.

When the doctor was through he just shook his head. Then the doctor said, "It's a wonder you ain't dead!"

Daddy broke his pelvis and seven ribs and his collar bone too. God was watching and saved his life that day.

Daddy was a Coal Miner and I am so proud.

The Guardian Angels stayed close for years until Jesus came to take him home at age 94.

So if your Daddy comes home from work with a black face, it is no disgrace.

My Daddy was a Coal Miner and I love him so.

Dahnmon's Little Stories

A tribute to Daddy from his family.
Located at the Coal Miners Memorial,.
Richlands, Virginia.

Dahnmon's Little Stories

Truitt Grist Mill

In the 1840's the little burg of Truittville was in need of a grist mill. Truittville was located in the Big White Oak Creek Valley of Greenup County, now on Kentucky Route 2070. Big White Oak Creek empties into Tygart Creek near Kentucky Route 7.

The main citizen of Truittville was Samuel Truitt. He was the Postmaster, ran a large farm, kept the Truitt Inn & Tavern, and also had a one man shoe factory ran by a Frenchman. Samuel was also a surveyor, teacher, and a medical doctor. Samuel never attended medical school; he was apprenticed under a medical doctor as was the case of most country doctors in the mid 1800's.

Truittville was quiet self-sufficient in most everyway except they had no grist mill. They had a creek full of water, but no mill-right to build the much needed grist mill.

Some how the blacksmith, Richard Devil Dick Whitt, from Gimlet Creek in Carter County met Samuel Truitt and heard of their plight. Richard told Samuel Truitt that his brother, Jonas Whitt over in Tazewell County, Virginia was a fine mill right and may consider making the trip to Kentucky for the purpose of constructing him a grist mill. Samuel was thrilled at the idea and wrote a letter promptly to Jonas Whitt, Baptist Valley, and Tazewell County, Virginia.

Jonas had just give up his wife, Susannah, with the birth of his last child. He was anxious to do something constructive and agreed to come to Greenup County and build Samuel Truitt a grist

Dahnmon's Little Stories

mill. In Jonas's reply to Samuel he explained that he had a son and a daughter both under the age of ten years old. He informed Samuel that he would need lodging and support to help with his children.

Samuel hurriedly replied to Jonas to bring his children to Kentucky. He explained that lodging would be provided as part of the pay. He even explained that he would teach the children during the construction period.

Jonas' children were David Crockett Whitt about ten years old and Henrietta (Hannah) about eight years old.

Jonas Whitt took Samuel Truitt up on his offer and traveled almost 200 miles with a wagon load of building tools, supplies, and his children. They traveled on the primitive roads and trails from Indian Creek, Baptist Valley, and Tazewell County, Virginia to Truittville, Greenup County, Kentucky. This took place around 1846 or 1847.

After Jonas arrived he surveyed the situation and determined to build an under-shot grist mill. To do this a trace or canal would have to be dug off of Big White Oak Creek to the mill and back to the creek. With an under-shot mill the flow of water is directed to the big mill wheel, striking it at the bottom and forcing it to turn, converting the power of the creek to power the grinding stone. The turning stone is about four feet in diameter and about one foot thick. The turning stone sets directly over the set stone of about the same size. These mill stones weigh upwards of a thousand pounds each. As grain is feed to the mill the grooved grinding stone is turned by the power of running water, thus grinding the corn or wheat.

Dahnmon's Little Stories

During the construction period Jonas Whitt and Mildred Truitt, Samuel's daughter, fell in love and were married on February 8, 1848 as registered in the records of Greenup County Courthouse. Jonas was about 24 years older than Mildred.

Hannah Whitt married Alfred Thompson on 12 June 1850, she was but thirteen years old. Her and Alfred, a lumber man, eventually moved to Lewis County where Hannah died in child birth with baby William Thompson about 1861.

David Crockett Whitt got into some trouble and hi-tailed it back to Virginia where he married Arminda Robinette. Crockett was a Confederate Soldier from 1862 until he was captured in the evening of April 8, 1865, only one day before General Lee surrendered.

Jonas ran the mill while teaching William Randolph Thompson the milling trade. A miller has much to learn about adjustments, safety, and caring for the mill. William Randolph Thompson became the principal miller in Truittville.

Jonas and Mildred had three sons, William Randolph Whitt, Jesse Monroe Whitt, and Alfred Jackson Whitt. William ended up with part of the property and it has been in the Whitt Family since the late 1800's. One of William Randolph Whitt's descendents Jesse Whitt owns the land now.

Jonas passed away on July 2nd 1865 and is buried in the woods on a little knoll overlooking Big White Oak Creek. I was raised in Tazewell County, Virginia and moved to Greenup County in 1970 having no idea that my great-great-grandfather, Jonas Whitt, was buried here in Greenup County, Kentucky.

I have not found out how long the mill was in operation. Not much evidence of the mill's

Dahnmon's Little Stories

existence other than a briar, weed, and brush filled trace where the water of Big White Oak Creek once flowed to power the mill.

From what I have learned the road that follows the creek up the valley, in the mid 1800's, once was considered a main road through Greenup County connecting the Tygert Valley with Lewis County. It is now Kentucky Route 2070.

The mill was located on the Jesse Whitt property, on Old Home Place Road, at a bridge passing over the Big White Oak Creek on Route 2070.

For a more detailed history, read the narrative, "Legacy, The Days of David Crockett Whitt." It is written by Colonel Charles Dahnmon Whitt and published with Jesse Stuart Foundation.

Dahnmon's Little Stories

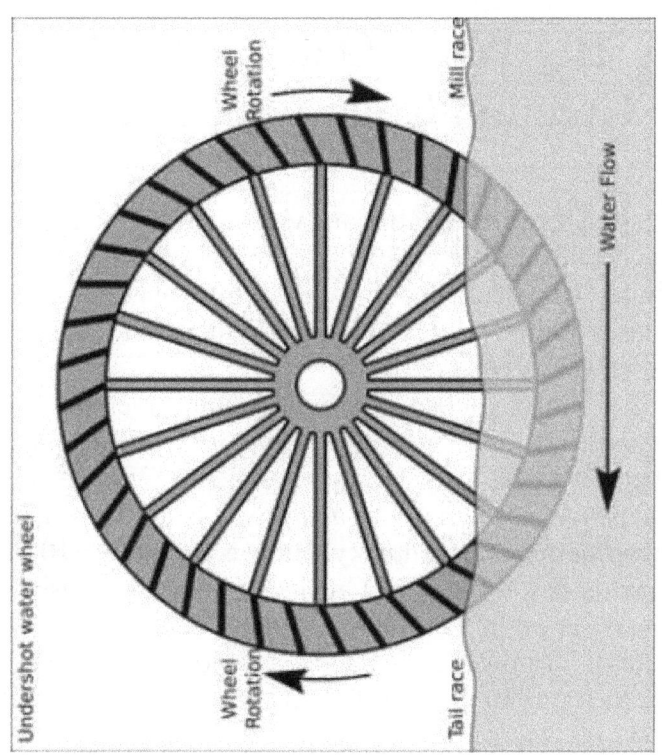

COLONEL CHARLES DAHNMON WHITT

Dahnmon's Little Stories

Big White Oak Creek of Greenup County Kentucky

Of course the Indians were the first to enjoy this beautiful little valley on the waters of Big White Oak Creek, and even had temporary villages there. The first white man to settle there that I can prove was James Gibbs.

James Gibbs was a Scotchman, a member of the crew on John Paul Jones' Bon Homme Richard when it met the British Serapis. After the War of Independence, James was awarded a land grant in the wilderness of Kentucky. He was awarded 3,100 acres on Big White Oak Creek. He build his house on a deserted Indian Village in the 1780's after the State of Virginia ceded Lands in Ohio and Kentucky to form military districts to be used as land grants to pay their soldiers and sailors for their service. James Gibbs owned most of the little valley on both sides of Big White Oak Creek.

James met his bride Mary Oliver the daughter of John Oliver and Mildred Fisher. Their daughter, Mary Elizabeth (Polly) Gibbs was born in 1786 in what is now Greenup County.

Mary Elizabeth met and married Dr. Samuel Truitt on May 25, 1818 in Greenup County. Samuel proved to be a worthy man with many talents. He was a medical doctor that gained his knowledge as an apprentice to another doctor. He never studied medicine in any medical schools. He was also a Surveyor, the first Post Master of Truittville, ran a water grist mill built by Jonas Whitt, ran a tannery and shoe factory with the help of a Frenchman from Canada. He also kept a large farm. He also kept an

Dahnmon's Little Stories

Inn that served travelers on the once busy road that followed Big White Oak Creek. Even though Samuel had all of these enterprises he found time to teach school to his children and the children of his employees.

Samuel Truitt could have very well been the first doctor and teacher in Greenup County. He was the founder of the little settlement named Truittville. He was the first Post Master of Truittville Post Office that lasted into the 1860's. The 1840 and 1850 Census was taken at the Truittville Post Office. Then the village was called Truitt. With the bigger towns along the Ohio River the traffic on the Truittville road decreased. Truitt is still part of the area, but York became the Post Office for a number of years. Now all the folks up and down the Big White Oak Creek get their mail delivered from South Shore, Kentucky.

There is much history in the little valley of Big White Oak Creek as can be verified by the many family cemeteries that dots the green hills all along the way. I discovered my GG Grandfather, Jonas Whitt's grave in one of these. He became a land owner in the early 1850's by marriage to Samuel Truitt's daughter, Mildred Truitt.

Truittville is long gone but I write this little history to keep her memory alive and to honor all the early settlers that helped build Greenup County Kentucky.

For more information please read the book, "Legacy, The Days Of David Crockett Whitt," written by me Colonel Charles Dahnmon Whitt.

Dahnmon's Little Stories

Chapter 35 Insert From the Book, "The Patriot, Hezekiah Whitt"

Tecumseh Stomps His Foot

The men at the Tazewell Court House in Jeffersonville talked and retold the stories of the great hero, William Henry Harrison, and how he demolished the Indian Confederation at Tippecanoe. Now if the British would just leave the United States alone.

In the year of 1811 Hezekiah received a letter from his father, Reverend Richard Whitt, which by reading between the lines Hezekiah could see his father was not doing too well. He decided he had better take the trip back to Meadow Creek while he could. The Indians were squelched for a time and Richard may not live too much longer. It was the time of harvest so he decided to leave the family home so he could travel faster and get back before the snows began. Jonas had not seen too much of Montgomery County and asked his father if he might go with him. Hezekiah asked if the Perry Mill could do with out him as he worked there most everyday. Jonas informed Hezekiah that he could get permission to go and he wanted to talk to grand paw Richard about mill building. You can go with me, but your grandfather may not be able to talk much about the mill. He told Jonas that his uncle, Archibald and others may be of some help. He told Jonas that the good Reverend may be really sick; after all he was 86 years old.

Dahnmon's Little Stories

Jonas was 15 years old and very handy with horses and at home in the woods. Hezekiah had taught all the boys about tracking and living off the land. He had given them a good education for the mountains of Virginia. Jonas as per most boys was not too happy to sit and learn the three "R's," but he faired well in his schooling. He wanted to be a mill right and carpenter and was handy with tools.

Hezekiah and Jonas headed toward Rocky Gap on November 15, 1811, it was a cold morning, and they both rode fine horses and had a pack mule to carry their gear. They made good time in the brisk air and were not too concerned with bandits and not at all with Indians.

They rose on November 16, 1811 and felt something they had never witnessed before. The earth shook under their feet and alarmed the horses. There were rocks rolling down the hills and the sky was filled with birds that were scared from their perches in the trees and bushes. A herd of deer bolted from the woods and almost ran over the Whitts, while they were trying to calm their horses.

"Paw, what on earth is happening?" asked an alarmed Jonas?

"It has to be an earthquake," said an excited Hezekiah.
"Paw, wasn't that the sign that Tecumseh said he would give, I thought they were all beaten by Harrison," said Jonas.

"Well son, I just don't pay too much attention to all the tales coming out of Indiana, I doubt this shaking of the earth has anything to do with that Indian," said Hezekiah trying to sound convincing.

COLONEL CHARLES DAHNMON WHITT

Dahnmon's Little Stories

"I sure hope it didn't brother anything back around home," said Jonas.

"Me to, we better get on the trail, I doubt it will happen any more," said Hezekiah.

Hezekiah and Jonas made good time and were in Meadow Creek on the big New River in a few days. They talked about the quake and wondered if it was just a local thing around Rocky Gap. Hezekiah and Jonas were greeted so warmly by the Whitts. The Reverend Richard had become so feeble, but still had a good mind. Things were so different to Hezekiah as he thought about the saying, "You cain't go home!"

Archibald's daughter Susannah was staying with the Reverend and Betsy Baxter Whitt and helping the aging couple. Susannah laid eyes on Jonas and his eyes met hers. There was a spark of electricity between the two. Jonas thought Susannah was the prettiest girl he had ever seen. Susannah was very attracted to Jonas. During the time they stayed in Meadow Creek Jonas made it his business to talk with Archibald and others about the mill work and mill building and of course this put him close to the lovely Susannah Whitt.

After a good visit with the Whitts and some of the Skaggs, Hezekiah and Jonas would start back home. The talk of the earthquake came up several times during the visit. The quake was even felt on Meadow Creek and had shaken an oil lamp from a neighbors table and set a fire, but they were home and quickly extinguished it. Another farmer had an old leaning barn fall to the ground. Hezekiah had prayed for God's protection on Rachel and the folks

Dahnmon's Little Stories

back in Tazewell County so with his great faith he left it to God.

Jonas and Susannah took a little walk in the woods the evening before their departure to say goodbye. They agreed to write and stay in touch and the two embraced and Susannah kissed Jonas passionately on the lips.

"Jonas, please come back to me," Susannah said quietly.

"I will, just as soon as I can, do you think your Paw and my other uncles will train me the work of mill building?" asked Jonas.

"Yes Jonas, I will write you often until you come back to me," said Susannah.

They finally tore lose from each other and the next morning Hezekiah and Jonas headed for Tazewell County. Susannah did not come out and bid Jonas goodbye, she was afraid that her true feelings would come out and she would cry and cling to Jonas. Hezekiah was really glad to visit his father and other family. Reverend Richard would do well to last through the winter.

The quake had hit in Tazewell County, but little damage occurred. It was bad enough for everyone to notice it and some damage was done here and there. As the Whitts rode into Hezekiah's Cedar Grove Rachel and the others ran to greet them. The first thing she said was, "Tecumseh's earthquake happened here, did y'all feel it on the trail?"

"We sure did Maw," blurted out Jonas.

Hezekiah gave him a look that spoke volumes. Jonas knew better than to talk when a question was to his father, but youth and excitement had played a hand.

"Sorry Paw," Jonas said quickly.

Hezekiah nodded approval and began to talk to Rachel after he had kissed and hugged his beloved princess.

Back on Tippecanoe River it was as if a bomb had gone off. The Indians saw that the Prophet had no real power and they scattered. A strong group of the Indians that were loyal to Tecumseh started a new village on Wildcat Creek. In the center of the new town was an ugly little Indian tied to a pole, it was the Prophet, Tenskwatawa.

The old village was pillaged by Harrison's army and burned. They found cases of brand new muskets that had been given by the British. There was nothing left of "Prophet Town".

Cheers went up as a party of Indians entered the town on Wildcat Creek. It was their beloved leader, Tecumseh and his faithful braves. Tecumseh stopped his horse abruptly and dismounted. His hardened eyes had spotted his brother. Tenskwatawa had hoped that Tecumseh would take pity on him, but his hope was dashed as he saw his livid brother walking toward him with a big skinning knife in his hand.

Tecumseh jerked Tenskwatawa's head around by gripping his hair. He laid the sharp blade to his exposed neck and pulled it slightly and drew a trickle of blood that slowly moved down to the base of his neck. Tenskwatawa thought he was dead fore sure! Tecumseh shoved him to the ground and stood

Dahnmon's Little Stories

to face his friends that had saved a remnant of his Confederation.

Death for the Prophet was too good, in a single day he had destroyed ten years of work. He had caused pain and coming destruction to all Indians as the great plan was all but broken. Tecumseh cast his brother out to be scorned. He was no longer the Prophet, not a brother, not an Indian, not even a man. Tenskwatawa would have neither family nor people; he would die a little each day until the demons of the underworld came for him.

Tecumseh would have to go to plan "B" and he hated it so badly. He would have to join the British against the seventeen fires. Tecumseh believed that many of the brave warriors that had lost hope could be brought back.

Tecumseh was still guided by the Great Spirit. Two signs had been given. The earth shook on December 16, 1811 and the Mississippi River ran backward for a time. The other sign was in the night sky, a great Comet of greenish light had passed through the sky (Remember that Tecumseh's name means panther crossing the sky as a comet did cross the sky the night the great man was born.) and now the tribes were to take the last red stick that had been given to almost all the tribes in two thirds of what is now the United States They cut it in to thirty pieces. A piece was burned each morning, now all was gone and the tribes would not have a fire until the great sign came. Indians to the far north, to the south to Florida, to the west beyond the Dakotas sat in the last night with no fire and waited. Of course the northern tribes were wrapped in blankets to ward off the winter cold. (Some of the tribes became know as the red stick people.)

COLONEL CHARLES DAHNMON WHITT

Dahnmon's Little Stories

On December 16, 1811 at about 2:30 AM, Tecumseh stomped his foot! The whole eastern half of the land now called the United States shook as if the Great Spirit was venting his anger. Tremors were felt all over America and it is still considered to be the strongest earthquake in history.

Creeks and lakes empted out and formed new paths and lakes, trees fell all over the land, huge boulders rolled down the mountains from Florida to way up in Canada. Reel Foot Lake on the Kentucky-Tennessee border was not a lake until on that faithful day when the earth shook so violently that millions of gallons of water spring up from the earth to form it. It is still there today. The Great Lakes churned with huge waves that came up over the highest banks. It shook as far as Yellowstone to the west. (Anvil Rock in Greenup County, Kentucky is documented as proof of this great sign. It lies at the foot of a hill near Lloyd, Kentucky to this day after rolling off the ridge above it.)

Wild animals and birds were scared from their beds and roosts, cattle in the fields fell to the ground. There was no doubt as to this great sign predicted by the great Chief Tecumseh. The center of the quake was near New Madrid, Missouri and is thought to be an 8 plus on the rector scale. This quake happened where there had never been one recorded before; no scientific explanation could be given. Only that the Great Tecumseh had stomped his foot.

There is no record to the lives lost or property destroyed, but if it happens today the cost may have been one million lives and billions of dollars lost in property. Memphis Tennessee would be leveled. Back in Tazewell County, Virginia many folks were

Dahnmon's Little Stories

shaken out of their beds and any weak structures hit the ground. Many rock houses in the cliffs of the mountains collapsed and some think that Swift's Silver Mine vanished this way.

The Whitts were up and quiet alarmed. Rachel spoke quietly to Hezekiah, trying not to scare the others in the house.

"It's Tecumseh's sign," she said.

Even Hezekiah knew something super natural was going on, could it be from God or could it be evil power from the devil?

The shaking on December 16, 1811 was only a starter. It lasted two full days and the sky was filled with a thick dust and smoke and even several days later the sun shown through a brown dingy sky.

Many folks got down and prayed for forgiveness as they thought the end times were upon them.

Indians all around knew that the Great Chief Tecumseh was not a liar and he was truly ruled by the Great Spirit. Many of the Indians that had ran away after the Tippecanoe battle now would began to come back to Tecumseh.

The British were thrilled with the new circumstances and that the Indians would truly be their ally. Now with their promise to the Indians that they would help drive the Americans back across the Blue Ridge Mountains, was what the Indians wanted to hear. The Indians would be ready to fight the Shemanese (White Men) when the British picked up the musket and tomahawk.

Was Tecumseh still stomping his foot? On January 23, 1812 another 7.8 earthquake hit near New Madrid, Missouri and again an 8.2 quake hit on

COLONEL CHARLES DAHNMON WHITT

Dahnmon's Little Stories

February 7, 1812. Each quake had loosened up the ground, rocks, and trees and the eastern half of what is now the United States was in a jumble. The last quake was the worst and did the most damage. Who could doubt Tecumseh now, after all he had given the prediction months before that the people would feel the earth shake when he stomped his foot.

Back in Tazewell County, Virginia the folks were thinking it must be close to the time that Jesus was coming back to claim His Church. Jesus had give warning as to the signs of His coming in Matthew Chapter 24: Verses 6-7.

> 6. *And you shall hear of wars and rumors of wars: see that ye be not troubled: for all these things must come to pass, but the end is not yet.*
> 7. *For nation shall rise against nation, and kingdom against kingdom: and there shall be famines, and pestilences, and earthquakes, in divers places.*

Hezekiah looked up this passage as it was so much on his mind. He read it to Rachel and some of the children that were around that evening.

"It sure looks like all of this is coming to pass," said Rachel.

"We are having wars and rumors all around the world and it looks like the British and the Indians are going to challenge us again," said Hezekiah.

"Yes it does and we sure have had the earthquakes and pestilences, and there are famines in some places," exclaimed Rachel.

Dahnmon's Little Stories

"We have to be ready for the wars and for the coming of our Lord," replied Hezekiah. Then he had a long prayer of praise, thanksgiving, and of repentance.

All we can do is pray, follow the Lord Jesus Christ and be ready to fight our enemies when they come.

Back in the Indiana territory the Indians that had deserted the cause because of the shortcomings of Tenskwatwa were now reconsidering Tecumseh as their leader against the Shemanese. Some thought it prudent to start the fighting where the nearest whites lived. They began to burn cabins, kill white folks and plunder their goods up and down the Wabash plumb to the Mississippi. Once again the settlers were going out prepared by carrying their muskets wherever they went, even out to get wood, water or work in their fields. The attacks spread to the State of Ohio and even some in Kentucky.

William Hull, the Governor of the new Michigan Territory was sending out scouts and getting nothing but bad news. The Indians were building up in big numbers and they all carried the new British Muskets. Hull was in contact with the government in Washington and asking congress to give permission to attack the Indians and British at Fort Malden. He urged the capture of Canada before the forces became too great.

President Madison authorized Hull and gave him the rank of General. He would send regular troops and call up 1,200 Ohio Militia and equip them with supplies and new blue uniforms with red collars. He also would provide a cocked hat with a white plume for each man.

Dahnmon's Little Stories

The headquarters were set up at Dayton, Ohio. Governor Meigs came to inspect the troops and meet with General Hull. They decided the best place to meet was in the McCullum's Tavern.

Now the new army of the northwest had 2,500 men and Hull accepted command from Governor Meigs. Hull had experience in soldering as he served with General Anthony Wayne during the Revolution. Hull felt very positive as he looked at his well dressed and well supplied army. Hull was not the man he was forty years ago. Now he was fat and sluggish and not the best man to be the leader. They marched on the first day of June, 1812 and in about six days reached Urbana. More local men joined the army as they marched toward the north.

Word spread like wild fire that the United States had declared war on Great Britain. Every able bodied man was ready to serve if called. President James Madison had been urging Congress for sometime to declare war. It was not just because of the Indians and British in the northwest, but the British had been boarding the American ships. The British had set up blockades to prevent goods to come or go to France and other countries. It was hurting the United States badly.

General Hull took his army toward Detroit and the going got rough because there were no real roads to the north. It took the army over two weeks to breach the Maumee River, only 95 miles distant. The men were exhausted and many of the horses and mules died from exhaustion of pulling wagons through brush and knee deep swamps.

General Hull took control of the United States Ship Cuyahoga and had all the supplies loaded aboard

COLONEL CHARLES DAHNMON WHITT

Dahnmon's Little Stories

her. He would send it ahead as he marched his army up the river. The General did the unthinkable thing of placing all of his papers and plans for the campaign on board. The Cuyahoga did not go too far before a British gunboat captured her and all of the supplies including Hull's plans. The information was forwarded to British General Isaac Brock.

Hull was unaware of this and his spies confirmed that Fort Malden was weak because reinforcements had not arrived. Hull commanded his army to move on Detroit, but when he got within about 15 miles he became plagued with the "what ifs". What if the attack cost many lives, what if the American General (Hull) was killed, what if Tecumseh unleashed his Indians on the settlers? Hull became so worried he turned his army back to Detroit, even though all the men were ready for a fight.

Back in Tazewell County the Whitts got word that the Reverend Richard Whitt had died. Hezekiah would take his family for a visit even though the old Patriarch would be long since buried. Edmund Whitt and Hannah Lestor Skaggs Whitt would take Rachel Rebecca Whitt age 9, Richard Price Whitt age 6., and little Abijah age 3 and travel with the Hezekiah party. Even some of the grown children would go on this trip to honor Richard Whitt. Griffy Whitt and wife Martha (Patty) Skaggs Whitt would go and take Timothy Whitt age 4, and Shone Whitt age 2. John Bunyan was not yet married and would also go. Rebecca Whitt Lowe was too much in the family way to travel; her Husband was John Husk Lowe. Little Calvin Lowe would be born in 1812. Susannah Whitt Webb and her husband Joseph Webb had no children as yet so they would also go.

COLONEL CHARLES DAHNMON WHITT

Dahnmon's Little Stories

Jonas was glad to go for another reason; he would get to see his Susannah again.

Reverend Richard Whitt's grown children that would be there were Robert, Abijah, Rachel, Elizabeth, Ruthy, Susannah, and Richard Thomas Whitt.

The trip was uneventful and that is what they wanted. The men carried their muskets across their saddles just in case the Indians or outlaws attacked. There was a great reunion as kindred came home to Meadow Creek to honor the good Reverend. They had an all night and all day Wake for their beloved Richard. They had a good time and laughed and cried. They all knew that the Old Reverend was walking around with Jesus and would want them to have a good visit as life is so short and they may never be all together again, at least here in this old world. Archibald took over as a leader during this time because he was the son that stayed home and took care of the Reverend during his declining years. After all the visits were over and folks were planning to go back home, Archibald brought out the will of the Reverend Richard Whitt and read it to everyone. He wanted all the folks to know what the Reverend's last will and testament was.

Richard Whitt, Sr. Will

25 April 1807
Montgomery County, Virginia
Will Book---? Pages 120-121

In the name of God I, Richard Whitt Senior of the County of Montgomery being in a feeble state of health, but sound of mind do ordain and declare this instrument of Writing to be my last Will and

Dahnmon's Little Stories

Testament Revoking all others. It is my wish after my death and for that purpose do will and bequeath to my son Archibald Whitt all the tract of Land whereon I now live and that the title shall fully be invested in him with all other claims that I may have to that and any other adjoining said tract to him and to his heirs forever. This tract is to be understood to contain the whole of the land that I bought from John Harrison on Meadow Creek supposed to be one hundred acres be it more or less to include the part which I have allotted to my son Richard at the upper end of said tract which son Archibald has bought and a title never was conveyed for it. I do also will to my beloved wife her equal one third of all my personal estate her natural life time the balance to be equally divided between my three daughters, Elizabeth Cassiday, Ruthy Whitt, & Susannah Creswell, and also should there be any part of wives Levasee left at her death also to be equally divided among my three daughters and their heirs forever. And for the good performance of my will and to execute the contents I appoint John Ingles & my son Archibald Whitt to act as executors and it is my request as I can place the fullest confidence in them that they shall act without being bond in security.

*Signed and subscribed to this my hand and seal this 25th day of April 18*Appointed as appraisers of personal property in 1813, were James Charlton, Jacob Peake, and William Sarles. The items including farm stock, produce, farm and household equipment. (log chains, lifter, log slide, drawing chain, 3 horses, which attest to the operation of "Whitt's Mill." A gray mare was listed at $40.00. Bearing proof to the education of the Whitts was

COLONEL CHARLES DAHNMON WHITT

Dahnmon's Little Stories

writing tablets, books, and 1 pair of spectacles and case. *(By James Whitt in 1983)*

There was much talk about the earthquakes and the war with Great Britain. Who knew what this would bring after a time of peace and great growth of the United States. All of the citizens thought that we would beat them again and put the savages down for good.

Jonas and Susannah spent all of their time together and fell even deeper in love. They really hated to part again and both promised themselves to each other. There would be a wedding someday, as Jonas promised to return and learn the mill building trade from his kindred, and take Susannah for his wife.

The Hezekiah party left after having a prayer for traveling mercies and of course praised God for His loving kindness. The trip back was basically fun and the beauty of southwest Virginia was enjoyed by all. Jonas was a little down, but the other Whitts kept making jokes and cheering him up. Hezekiah even explained to him that if it is meant to be, it will happen.

Dahnmon's Little Stories

The Author

Colonel Charles Dahnmon Whitt Author Of:
"Legacy, The Days Of David Crockett Whitt"

"The Patriot, Hezekiah Whitt"

"Dahnmon's Little Stories"

     Whitt a native of Tazewell County, Virginia moved to Kentucky in 1970 to carry out his trade as a Sheet Metal Worker with Local 24, Southern Ohio. Although he is now retired, he has always had an interest in genealogy and was always a real history buff for regional and civil war history; however, he didn't pursue his interest until he started researching his ancestry on-line in 1999.
     While tracing his family's heritage, Whitt was soon introduced to his great-grandfather David Crockett Whitt. Yes, the discoveries that he had made during his fascinating search led

Dahnmon's Little Stories

him to create "Legacy, The Days of David Crockett Whitt," a work of historical fiction with his great-grandfather serving as the skeleton for this account of life in an earlier, and harder time 1836-1900

Legacy follows Whitt's great-grandfather "Crockett," through the early settler days in Virginia and Kentucky from 1836 thru 1909, his formative years in Greenup County Kentucky and the time that he spent in a Civil War prison.

Whitt has now written another book, "The Patriot, Hezekiah Whitt," which deals with the years of 1760 -1846. Hezekiah Whitt was a founding father of Tazewell County, Virginia. He was a Militiaman, Indian Spy, Sheriff, and a lifelong Gentlemen Justice of the Peace appointed by the Governor of Virginia. Hezekiah Whitt is Whitt's GGG Grandfather. This book abounds with Indian stories.

In "Legacy, The Days Of David Crockett Whitt" and "The Patriot, Hezekiah Whitt" you will soon discover when acquainting yourself with these particular titles is that Whitt encompasses his faith and shows these pioneer families relying on their faith as well to get through trying times.

Charles is able to use the prefix "Colonel" in his pen-name because he is a Kentucky Colonel.

Dahnmon's Little Stories

Colonel Whitt has also written a smaller fun book called, "Dahnmon's Little Stories," which is a collection of short stories and poems. Price is $10.00 for it, plus shipping is $4.00. (Paper Back)
To purchase these books go to http://dahnmonwhittfamily.com or for a signed book, write to Post Office Box 831, Flatwoods, KY. 41139. Price for these researched hardback books is $30. Plus $6 when shipping is required. Published and sold by Jesse Stuart Foundation in Ashland, Kentucky. My Phone # 606 836 7997   E-Mail c-dahnmon@roadrunner.com

Dahnmon's Little Stories

**The Old Colonel
Charles Dahnmon Whitt
Confederate History is American
History**

www.ingramcontent.com/pod-product-compliance
Lightning Source LLC
Chambersburg PA
CBHW032140040426
42449CB00005B/333